HARDPRESS.NET
HOME OF HARD-TO-FIND BOOKS

O'hara; Or, 1798
by William Hamilton Maxwell

Address:
HardPress
8345 NW 66TH ST #2561
MIAMI FL 33166-2626
USA
Email: info@hardpress.net

C. v. +. Isaruche. —

O'HARA;

OR,

1798.

"Non enim propter gloriam divitias aut honores pugnamus sed propter libertatem solummodo quam nemo bonus nisi simul cum vita amittit." —LIT. AD PAP. A.D. 1820.

"Guilty as many of those were on whom the heavy vengeance of the Government descended, it is melancholy to think that they were not the most guilty."—EDIN. REVIEW, 1811.

IN TWO VOLUMES.

VOL. I.

London:

PRINTED FOR

J. ANDREWS, 167, NEW BOND-STREET;
AND MILIKEN, DUBLIN.

MDCCCXXV.

LONDON
PRINTED BY WILLIAM CLOWES,
Northumberland-court.

" What a noble fellow," said Lord Byron, after I had finished reading, " was Lord Edward Fitzgerald, and what a romantic and singular history was his! If it were not too near our times, it would make the finest subject in the world for an historical Novel."

MEDWIN's *Conversations of Byron*, p. 220.

INTRODUCTION.

To Sir John Bridgworth, Bart.

Banville, October 26, 1815.

You are no little astonished that one, not to say in robust health, should venture to cross the Irish Channel, at this advanced season, in a crazy, ill-found packet, and that my Belgic trip had not been quite enough for this year of 1815.

As I intend to acquaint you with the causes of this sudden excursion, I feel it will be necessary to give you some account of myself; all of my earlier history that you know is, that I am an Irishman, and I presume you suspect an obscure one. In this conjecture you would be quite correct; but, without further preface, I will tell you my simple story :—

I was born in the north of Ireland; my father was an honest miller, that is, conditionally, as any other of the trade; and my mother a hard-working, thrifty housewife: both were industrious, and, of course, the good man became wealthy. My infancy was unmarked by any thing of importance; and I remember my first fifteen years passed with all the sameness of the quiet river which rolled before our door, and the only events which gave me joy or sorrow, were those connected with the humblest scenes of life. My father and mother were ever grumbling about something; but still the neighbours said, no matter whose gear was dwindling away, that theirs was increasing. The kiln-fire was the rendezvous of all tatlers and newsmongers;

there every lament was made, and there the complainant was certain, especially if the night was cold, to have a large and attentive auditory ; my father ever looked at the gloomy side of the picture, and if it so happened, which in truth was rare, that he had nothing lugubrious to commence with, he looked sorrowful, and sat in moody silence. It was, however, but seldom that he was reduced to this dilemma ; if the crops were indifferent, he predicted famine for the populace ; if they promised to be abundant, he denounced bankruptcy to the farmer ; one while the country would be starved, and at another the grain would be for the lifting. In politics, he was equally unhappy ; and whenever a newspaper made its way from the castle-kitchen to the kiln-fire, it had surely something of fearful import in its greasy columns. When a privateer was seen in the Channel, my father prognosticated an invasion ; and

a burglary occurring at the other side of
the kingdom, gave him a glorious opportunity of calculating what chances were
in favour of having his throat cut.

In this agreeable and instructive society my evenings were consumed, and
if any interruption took place in the
melancholy details of the night, imagination filled.

Each dreary pause between

with what had more effect on me than
the most pathetic of the miseries of my
worthy parent. The morning, and the
Village Schoolmaster, flashed across my
mind, and there was, indeed, nothing
exhilarating in the idea. Peter Martin
carried terror in his name, and Heaven
knows with good reason : in his youth
he was reckoned stern, but now, that
age and domestic calamities had over-
taken him, he was absolutely savage;
he regularly opened the campaign by
flogging me and my companions every

morning on our entré to the academy; and his ingenuity was amazing in what a Lawyer would call " shewing cause why :"—a duck lamed, or a hen dying a natural death, was reckoned good and sufficient grounds for a general visitation; and as practice makes perfect, the rapidity with which the point of honour was settled between all parties was prodigious. The baker's son, a tall overgrown booby, was an experienced assistant; and at this moment I fancy myself dangling on his long back, with my head turned half round, trembling as I watched the impending blow.

Peter Martin was a humorist of a peculiar cast; he had a by-name for every scholar, and he gave a pleasant variety to his favourite discipline by the facetious use of the individual's appellative. This liberality of birch was not, however, attended with a corresponding proficiency in erudition—the harder

Peter flogged, the less progress the pupils made. The coercive system had a very opposite effect to what the pedagogue supposed it would produce. The wilder boys became devils—the quieter became wild. Peter, like a liberal paymaster, endeavoured to be always in advance with them; and they, not to be outdone, laboured hard in all mischief, to keep the account tolerably even on all sides.

Six years had I dragged on, when an incident occurred which dissolved the connexion between Peter Martin and myself. The Dissenting Minister of our parish, the Rev. Samuel Gowdy, dined occasionally at the Mill; and, at his particular recommendation, my father decided on breeding me up to the Ministry. "The lad's springing up fast," said the Rev. Gentleman to my father, "and in a few years ye must send him over the water to the College. What has he

learned from Martin, good man?" That was a question my father honestly acknowledged he could not answer, and Gowdy was entreated to ascertain the extent of my acquirements. I was accordingly summoned into the presence, and the result was most unfavourable. " Before God, friend David," said the Minister to my father, " Bob knows nothing." Peter Martin, when informed of the fatal discovery, ascribed my deficiencies to excessive indulgence and a blamable tenderness on his part, and quoted the old adage, " spare rod and spoil child ;" he declared, however, he would turn over a new leaf with me, and I had soon certain proof that he made no empty professions—formerly, I had escaped with being disciplined once a day, but now, to make up for past lenity, the average was increased threefold. My mother observed, that of late any posture was preferred by me to a sitting one;

and, on discovering the extent of my sufferings, betrayed a sympathy I could not have expected from her. This encouraged me so much, that, on the following day, when a grand elevation of the Disciples, *en masse*, was to take place for the alleged fracture of a sky-light, (which, by-the-by, was broken by the storm,) and my turn for bestriding the baker's son arrived, I snatched up my hat, and ran for it. This was a crime for which there was no forgiveness; it was totally without the pale of mercy, and with me the Rubicon was passed. On looking behind me, I saw Martin's prime-minister, the young baker, at my heels; the mill, fortunately, was near——I dashed up stairs, and never reckoned myself secure from pursuit till I had clambered up the roof, and perched myself on the ridge-tiles. I was soon summoned to surrender; the noise brought my mother to the door, who, on seeing my dangerous position, screamed lustily for my father. In vain were threats and entreaties used; I knew well what I had to expect from Martin, and determined to hold out to the last extremity. Gowdy fortunately at this time happened to be passing; my parents acquainted him with the affair, and my mother enlarged on the striking marks of Peter's discipline which my person incontestibly avouched. A capitulation was proposed by the Divine; I was emancipated from Martin's clutches, the baker's son was dismissed in disgrace, and with a lightened heart I descended briskly from my airy resting-place.

A difficulty now occurred as to whose care I should be committed: Gowdy recommended a neighbouring Minister, and on application being accordingly made, he undertook to prepare me for the Scotch University. He was a man of mild and winning manners, and de-

servedly reckoned one of the most accomplished scholars of the day. His
circumstances were considered tolerably comfortable; and occupation and society, more than pecuniary emolument,
formed his chief inducements for receiving me and another; of that other I shall
have occasion to speak much——he was in
after life an instance of the mutability of
fortune, and the uncertainty of human
happiness; in short, my fellow-student
under the roof of Doctor Graham, was
the once-celebrated Frederic O'Hara.

O'Hara was one year older than I,
but the difference between us was
every way disproportionate. I was
rather small and delicate for my years
——he was stout, well made, and well
grown——he was devoted to all kinds of
field sports, while I was rather inclined
to be sedentary and inactive. On the
mountains he usually tired two or three
sets of dogs, and me most heartily when

I accompanied him (which indeed was seldom); and on our return home, when with difficulty I dragged my wearied legs up the steep ascent which led to the Doctor's door, O'Hara would sit down quietly to dinner in his wet clothes, and after despatching a formidable meal, change his dress, mount his horse, and ride six miles to the monthly assembly, and dance till day-light; while I, tired to death, crawled to my bed with difficulty. His superiority over me in physical strength was but proportionable to his mental pre-eminence. With such dispositions as I have described, a want of application might be expected; he read very little, but he remembered that little; and the brilliancy of his natural talents amply compensated for a total absence of industry. He was intended for the bar, but his father turned very little of his attention to what should be the future object of his son's pursuits.

He was the most indolent and the most
hospitable being in the world ; and the
only earthly thing he seemed to be interested in, was keeping Castle Carra
(the venerable seat of his ancestors) in
repair.   The house was ever full of company—the consumption of provisions
and liquors was enormous, for the kitchen
was crammed full of servants, and what
the Irish call coucherers (hangers on),
and the stables crowded with horses and
dogs.   The remains of the family estates
which had descended to him, and which,
with common care, might have become
a fine and valuable inheritance for his
child, were hourly passing piece-meal
into other hands, when, luckily for
my young companion, an apoplexy removed Anthony O'Hara, but not till he
had alienated all the property, except a
small portion which was strictly entailed.
Early the same year, I lost my mother ;
and the ensuing autumn my father fell a

victim to an epidemic then prevailing in the country. I had never been friendly to the choice of profession made for me by my parents; and now, having become my own master at the early age of eighteen, I selected physic for my future pursuit.

A circumstance occurred at this time that marked Frederic's character, and in a great measure decided his professional selection. A younger brother of his deceased father, who had been, I believe, a captain in the Irish Brigade, was returning from France. When within a day's journey of home, he accidentally met some military persons: a quarrel and duel ensued, and unfortunately Captain O'Hara fell (as it was generally supposed) unfairly. I remember the evening he was interred in the burying-ground of the Castle Carra family. I saw a message delivered to Frederic O'Hara, who acted as chief mourner; and, to the astonishment of

all, he left the funeral while the clergyman was still engaged in the solemn
service of the dead. All were conjectur-
ing the cause of this extraordinary departure, when we saw the object of our
surmises riding hastily along the shores
of the lake, followed by his groom. Three
hours dispelled the mystery—the antagonist of his uncle had rested at the
town of Newbridge, and O'Hara hastily
rode off to meet him. An immediate
duel was the consequence; it was fought
by candlelight in the parlour of the inn.
One discharge of pistols decided all.
O'Hara was slightly wounded, but Mac-
kinnon (I think that was the name) was
killed upon the spot.

Frederic O'Hara came to visit me,
and we freely communicated on our
respective affairs; he told me his father
had made a lamentable inroad into what
had escaped the casualties of former
days; and that he had determined on
entering the army, as the remaining pro-

perty was too trifling to support so expensive an establishment as that of Castle Carra. To his only surviving uncle, he proposed consigning the arrangement of his shattered inheritance, and as he was an opposite to his late brother, O'Hara hoped every thing from his arrangement.

We took leave then, never to meet again. He hastened to London, and I to the Irish capital, where, after residing the necessary time, I took my degrees, and went to finish my studies at Leyden; with the remainder of my common-place kind of life you are sufficiently acquainted. I went professionally to India; and there the meridian of my days was spent. If I was not the most skilful of physicians, I was certainly an attentive one: I was lucky enough to make a name, and that name made my fortune. I returned to England after an absence of thirty-five years, and, on inquiry, learned that not even the remotest of my relatives was in existence. Some had emigrated, and others died, in the long period of my absence: the few friends of my youth were next sought after, and I found myself equally bereft of all.

Doctor Graham had written for several years to me; but death, in common course, deprived me of my venerated correspondent. From Frederic O'Hara I had heard twice or thrice: the last letter acquainted me with his marriage, and the newspapers with his going on foreign service. From that period, I only occasionally saw his name in the columns of the public journals—sometimes mentioned with applause, at others loaded with abuse, according to the temper of the times, or the political complexion of the paper. As he advanced in life, I remarked him more frequently brought forward; and at length becoming fatally conspicuous as a revolutionary leader, and in the eventful year of 1798, his death, and the exile of his only son, seemed to have concluded the history and the existence of his family ; for excepting some few casual notices of the latter, I never saw the name again recorded. I conjectured that the fortunes of the O'Haras had been sadly reduced ; but on my return to Europe, I found my worst fears for the child of my quondam friend confirmed :——the ancient house had fallen, the very name was annihilated, and the buildings which had sheltered them for ages, was now a ruined pile.

From some of my countrymen, whom I met occasionally in London, I learned many particulars, and among others, that the existence of the younger O'Hara was still a matter of uncertainty. He had, after the death of his father, openly declared against the Government, and held a principal command in the fatal battles of Antrim and Ballinahinch. On the total defeat of the Northern Rebels, he had been left a solitary wanderer; and, after many romantic exploits, succeeded in escaping pursuit; left the kingdom, and entered the service of the French Republic. He had been seen in Paris in 1803, then bearing a Captain's commission; but, from that time, no one had heard of or seen him, and it was a general opinion that he had fallen in some of Buonaparte's campaigns; but of his being dead or living, there was no certainty.

To ascertain the fate of Henry O'Hara; to take him, if living, from obscurity and distress——to restore the fallen name, and raise again the fortunes of his house, formed the future objects of the Miller's son; and, in prosecution of my plan, I forthwith left London for the Continent. The fatal return of that extraordinary spirit from his temporary captivity, convulsed and agitated Europe ; my career, like that of greater men, was arrested by it, and being compelled to remain in Belgium, waiting for happier times, I selected Brussels as a place where I might prosecute my inquiries when barred from entering the French territories. Wonderful and rapid events succeeded, till once more the fatal field of Waterloo consigned Napoleon to exile.

I was reading on the night of the 14th in my chamber—the late Colonel ——, of the Artillery, a countryman of mine, lived in the same hotel ; we became intimate in a short time ; he was a fine soldier, and a charming companion : I had told him generally, I was come to make inquiries after a relative in the French service. When the alarm sounded on that night, my brave friend hurried from the ball-room to the field —he passed my chamber on leaving his own, where he had been making some trifling alterations in his dress, and perceiving by my yet unextinguished light that I was awake, he called to take leave of me—poor fellow!—it was an eternal adieu! He jocularly asked me, how should he know my friend in the French ranks, that he might have the honour of measuring swords with him? His jest might have turned out a reality; for both fought, and both fell, at Waterloo! I shall only remark, that here ended my hopes and fears, and with them all my future objects. I had found the last of the O'Haras only to lay him in the earth. My late friend, the Colonel, rests in the same grave ; I laid them by each other's side, and one small mound of turf covers the gallant foemen.

Thus terminated my castle-building ; but as all I heard of this extraordinary man (young O'Hara) only raised without satisfying my curiosity, I determined on a pilgrimage to the scenes of his youth.

This was my inducement for my late excursion to the land of Saints, and I will now proceed to tell you how far I have succeeded in my object.

I landed safely in Dublin—Alas! how changed! I shall not, however, dwell on the causes which ruined this noble city. I leave it with a sigh "fuit Ilium." From Dublin, I directed my course northerly; and the rapidity with which The Fly (as the vehicle was termed) bore me to my destination, compared with the old lumbering coach or caravan which had conveyed me from my home, probably gave rise to conjectures that I should find every thing generally and proportionately altered. They were altered, but, unfortunately, not for the better. When I last travelled this road, the Northern bleachers were a prosperous and numerous body; but now, the usual reply to my inquiry of what each ruined edifice had been, was " a bleach-mill," or " a manufactory." Some of the proprietors I had personally known—they were enterprising and wealthy, accumulating riches themselves, and disseminating money throughout a happy and contented community. I remembered well that the linen trade was preferred by the estated gentry of my neighbourhood, as affording to their sons a respectable, and a more certain livelihood than any of the honourable or learned professions to which men of family usually devoted their younger children; but that class, I learned, had long since retired from the ruins of a hopeless trade; while those whose fathers had expended fortunes, the fruits of long and successful industry, in erecting expensive machinery, with houses for the hundreds they employed —those men, unable to free themselves from the business with which their all was compromised, unable to escape an impending danger which all foresaw, but none could avert, sat in their cheerless homes, each year more hopeless than the last, each chance of ultimate relief more desperate, till at length the honest earnings of parental industry were no more, and bankruptcy consigned to penury and despair those who were ever industrious, and, alas! had once been opulent.

In the evening, I reached the town of N——, and on the following day left it for the village of M——, where the first years of my life had been passed. It was the market-day when the postillion stopped at the little inn, but all that indicated this day of business and bustle was a string of beggarly apple-stalls, and a few wretched old women, with scanty bunches of yarn, huddled together in a corner of the square. Few as the sellers were, and limited as was the quantity of their commodity, they seemed far to exceed the demand. The market-house was in a ruinous state; the little cupola still bore the dial of the town-clock, which for many years had ceased to tell the flight of time—the rusted hand pointed to the tenth hour, and its association recalled " days of lang syne." I looked for the academy of Peter Martin—it was roofless. How often, as I hurried to his house, has my course been impeded in the very spot I stood in; when the now silent bell struck the hour to which the idle hand still pointed, hundreds sprung up and towered above the crowd, while a thousand lusty arms instantly exhibited their merchandise. To understand me, you must be aware of what an Irish Linen Market *was ;*—the buyers occupied benches, which raised them some feet above those who sold: the sale commenced as the town-clock told the hour; and at the first beat of the bell, the merchants leaping on their forms, and the instantaneous protrusion of some thousand webs for their inspection, seemed almost magical.

The inn at which I stopped was, in the days of its prosperity, the lowest of the village Hostels—its humbleness had probably been the cause of its lingering beyond its competitors. I looked up the street for my old acquaintance, the Jolly Draper—the Jolly Draper had disappeared. Where were the Red Lion, and the Black Bear, and the White Swan? All gone. I looked in vain for some house whose fairer external would promise better accommodation than the General Wolfe; none but some wretched pot-houses were visible: I had no choice, and into the General Wolfe I entered with a heavy heart.

Although the gallant commander had contrived to outlive his competitors for public favour, he was evidently on the point of annihilation; all within was filthy and comfortless—the earthen floor of the kitchen was deeply furrowed with holes, and what each of these pits wanted in clay, they seemed to have supplied with water; with no inconsiderable difficulty I piloted myself clear of the numerous pools, to where an old dirty-looking wo- man was bent double across the smoky embers. I asked if I could get accommo- dation and a chamber? " *E-agh,*" was thrice replied to my inquiries; a third demand, with a considerable intonation of voice, brought a ragged, red-headed girl to the stair-head, who peeping over the crazy bannister, kept bawling at the same time, " Wolly, here's a gentleman, shake yourself, mun, and turn the pig out of the parlour." Wolly presently showed himself; he had, I presume, been sleeping, as he yawned every step he made in his descent, when he presented to my view a dozed, drunken, stupid sot of forty—his face swollen and flaccid, his eye dim and reeling; and yet the features were the very counterpart of an old acquaintance, his father. How different, and yet how much alike. The father an active, thrifty publican—the son a wretched, bloated pauper! The sot inducted me to the sitting-room—it was in unison with the kitchen; the table bore the marks of the last night's revels of some carriers who were driving from the door; beer was splashed over the seats, broken pipes and pewter measures were everywhere strewn around. I, however, yielding to necessity, endeavoured to make my misfortunes as light as I could; I raised one window, (the other was built up with loose stones to save the tax,) set the sandy-haired drab to scrub, and having ordered breakfast, strolled out, glad to escape an atmosphere tainted with whiskey and bad tobacco. Need I describe my farther investigation of this "deserted village?" In a word, I had put up at the best

house ; and from it you can estimate
what kind the inferior ones must have
been. A sickening stroll of half an hour
led me through filth, misery, and dilapi-
dation ; and having perceived the frequent excursions of " the Maid of the
Inn," from her own château to the adjacent hovels, from which she appeared
to be gleaning the necessary articles for
my consumption, I re-entered the General Wolfe. You may suppose I did not
dally over my morning repast, yet it required some longer time than I had calculated; the table equipage had severally
to undergo ablution, and God knows I
was not fastidious in my cleanliness,
after all. I was miserable till I found
myself once more in the open air.

I cannot describe my feelings as I bent
my steps towards the Mill : the road by
which I left the town was bad and rugged ; an ill-constructed splash-wall (the
Irish name for a loose, thin fence of

stones, placed at random upon each other) was all that divided the highway from the adjacent fields—not a tree, not a bush was visible. Many a time have I walked to Peter Martin's academy through an avenue, sheltered on either side by hawthorn hedges, and canopied above by ashen boughs; I was now striding over a bare and broken causeway. I hurried over the short mile which divided my father's house from the village. I stood above the little quiet valley where my parents had drawn their first breath, and where their last sigh had been breathed. I looked for the mill, the farm-yard, and the garden; but I looked in vain—like those who had occupied them, they were gone: I seated myself on a bank above them, and wept bitterly; a step startled me, and broke in upon my sorrow—a middle-aged, decent yeoman stood beside me, and in-

quired, with a solicitude free from all
appearance of impertinence, if I was
unwell? I replied in the negative, and
told him I was a stranger, affected after
a long absence, by seeing places once
familiar to me. His house was beside-
us, and he invited me to enter it. It
was a clean, commodious dwelling, well
slated, and in good repair, and, as I remember, occupied the spot where our
old kiln-man's cottage stood. From the
door I looked if I could possibly discover
the foundation of my father's dwelling;
but the ground on which it had been
erected was now covered by a decayed
brewery. The little gig-mill which had
made my father's livelihood, had been
removed, and its site occupied by a spacious bleach-mill. The topographical
appearance of all around was altered,
the fences having been taken away to
make room for the bleaching-grounds.

"There is a great change here, no doubt, within your memory," said my new acquaintance.

"There is, indeed," said I, with a heavy sigh.

"How long is it, may I ask, since you were last here?"

"Five and thirty long years."

He seemed astonished. "Why then you remember old Ashworth's gig-mill, and his house, and——"

"All—all; they have given place to those modern buildings——"

"My father," said the man pulled them down."

"What? was Thomas Morgan your father?"

"No—my father purchased this place in an unlucky hour from Morgan."

Mutual inquiries produced a mutual recognition. Stephens seemed delighted to have met with an acquaintance of his father's; and while dinner was preparing, we seated ourselves on a bench before the door, and he communicated particulars of which I was uninformed.

"My father, you know, was wealthy; he had three sons, of whom I am the youngest, and the sole survivor; my eldest brother was apprenticed to the linen trade, the second he intended for an attorney, and I was destined to be a brewer. The linen trade was then prosperous, and offered the fairest prospects of future opulence to those who embarked in its manufacture. In it my father unfortunately speculated deeply, at the suggestion of my eldest brother, and so assured was he of the stability of that trade, that, contrary to his own desire, he brought my second brother home, and placed him in partnership with himself. In order to promote the greater extension of his business, he purchased this property, and erected the mills which you see, and which, alas! are falling rapidly into decay.

" For some short time my family prospered in their business, but, like all others, they were fated to meet with ultimate disappointment. My second brother was what is usually termed eccentric, and not being so sanguine of success as his brother, greatly assisted, by constant opposition to extensive speculation, to keep the house in safety, although their profits were but moderate.

" Thus fared my father and my brothers, till at length the politics of these unhappy times led to a lamented crisis. My second brother preferred the ruinous course of revolutionary principles to that of abject and bigoted subserviency to the government. He possessed some talent, and unluckily for himself and his family, it was devoted to the cause of constitutional reform. His associates were all marked and prominent cha-

c

racters, and though my brother was too mild and too gentle to take a share in any overt act of hostility; yet, implicated with the more desperate, and identified with the active, he was obliged to leave the country at a moment when his influence was more than ever required to restrain the unsuccessful speculations of his brother. The sequel comes within my own knowledge ; my eldest brother, unrestricted in his wild schemes, launched deeper into a falling commodity, and that wealth which had been for years in our possession, melted rapidly away. My father, heart-broken by the imprudence of his eldest, and the exile of his second son, died—while he, the cause of all, although absent from his home, endeavoured to break the fatal mercantile spirit of his brother—it was unavailing, he plunged farther into the ebbing tide, and when at the very brink of bankruptcy, died of a fever, before his mis-

fortunes were consummated by a pro-
claimed insolvency.

"About this time the government permitted my brother to return, and having
arranged the debts of the deceased, he
formed a partnership with me, and endeavoured to turn the mills to some
account. I need not be very particular
as to the result; ten years we lingered
on, and all that our united prudence and
economy could do, was to keep ourselves from appearing in the Gazette.
At length my brother's health began to
decline, no doubt occasioned by mental
anxiety and bodily fatigue, for which he
was unfitted, and we came to a resolution to sell this place, and live on the
produce of the sale. We did so, but at
a prodigious loss; and yet the present
proprietor heavily regrets the purchase.

"Prior to the rebellion, my brother
had been induced to cultivate his literary
acquirements from his intimacy with

the O'Haras." I interrupted him—"Do you know any thing of them, and particularly the younger?"

" Much—more than any other man in existence. I would explain myself more fully. When the elder suffered, his son effected an escape to France; my brother, as I told you, was his companion; they met, and lived together till the military profession of young O'Hara obliged him to join the army of Italy. The amnesty which included my brother's name was issued before they met again, and knowing the urgency of our affairs here, he left Paris without a moment's delay, when assured that the clemency of the Crown was extended to him. From young O'Hara he had received a faithful narrative of his numerous adventures, and to the period of his death occasionally had letters from him. During the declining years of his life, my brother remained in Dublin ; for, labouring under an organic disease, it was necessary to be near experienced physicians ; and for a long time previous to his dissolution, he amused the solitude of a sick chamber by arranging the letters and compiling a memoir of his absent friend. Whether he ever proposed giving them to the world is very questionable ; for, as many of the actors in these lamented scenes were still upon the stage, the memoirs of Henry O'Hara must of necessity have involved their histories."

I had now found all I wished—of course I acquainted him with the sole object of my expedition, and of the death of the *last of the O'Haras*. All that I desired he granted—a perusal of his brother's manuscript. He also accommodated me with a chamber in his house, and my present employments are—a daily pilgrimage to the ruins of Castle Carra, while my evenings pass away in transcribing the memoirs of its last owner. When my task is completed, I will forward it to you, and for ever bid good bye to this unhappy, but lovely island. Forgive the formidable dimensions of this packet, and present my regards to your lady and her daughters.

Believe me, my dear Bridgworth,
ever faithfully your friend,
ROBERT ASHWORTH.

Banville, Nov. 28th, 1815.

My dear Bridgworth,

I RECEIVED your letter of the tenth, and shall feel great happiness in making one of your Christmas circle. I am heart-sick of this once-loved spot, although all that poor Stephens and his amiable family can do for my comfort is done. I have performed my task, and the little history of Henry O'Hara is completed ; it shall be at your service at Bridgworth.

I have made my last pilgrimage to Castle Carra, and amidst its desolation paid the tribute of a tear to the memory of its hapless owners. When I left my native valley, the seat of Frederic O'Hara enticed the traveller to digress from the direct road, and repaid him by its noble and ancient grandeur. What now meets his eye?—a pile of scorched buildings—roofless and grass-grown—nothing left but the oaken and scathed beams which supported the lofty ceilings, and which, from their size and solidity, bade defiance to the devouring element—of all its noble oaks not one remains to screen the traveller from the shower. The gothic fury of the bigot yeomen consigned the building to the flames, while the lands escheated to the Crown were left without one tree to shelter them. The lawn and gardens are now in little patches of tillage, and along the sweet banks of the mountain rivulet, once almost concealed by full grown evergreens, the boors have placed their mud-walled cabins, and the old curse may be considered as fulfilled on the name of O'Hara,

> The hare may shelter in his hall.

I intend to go to Dublin on Thursday, and without delay to embark for England, where I hope to find that peace which would be now unattainable in this my native island. Adieu,

> Dear Bridgworth, ever yours,
> ROBERT ASHWORTH.

Gresham's Hotel, Nov. 30th.

P. S. I detained my letter until this post in order to fix my departure with certainty. I am to leave Dublin this evening in the Holyhead Packet, and may well say with the Poet,

> My native land, Good night,
> R. A,

O'HARA.

CHAPTER I.

Come thy summons when it may,
Thou wilt not leave a braver man behind.
Southey's Madoc.

IT was a clear cold morning in February—the
47th Regiment was drawn up for parade on the
Mall, and the officers were falling into line, as
old Colonel Abercrombie rode up on his white
charger. Time had changed the colour of the
steed from light grey to milky whiteness; the
horse and his rider were old friends, and
many a day's service had they seen together.
That something uncommon had occurred was
quickly observed by the regiment; for the Colonel sat more erect, and the charger moved

with more than usual animation: conjecture was, however, soon put to rest by the veteran's producing a packet of War-office dimensions, which, on reaching the centre of the line, he opened with suitable solemnity—all was breathless attention. The Colonel hemmed twice— " Forty-seventh regiment,"—" His Majesty (God bless him!) has deigned to confer high honour on the corps I command, by selecting them for foreign service—I have here orders of readiness for America: the officers, non-commissioned officers, and privates will, therefore, prepare every thing for speedy embarkation. In my person,"—the Colonel hemmed again— " his Majesty has honoured me with his gracious consideration, by signifying his intention of giving me a command at home, should I apprehend my health would suffer by change of climate; but, I am now well stricken in years, and where can I die so happily as with that regiment which for twenty-five years it was my pride to serve in?" The unequal voice with which this short speech concluded, showed how full the Colonel's heart was; and, as he uncovered his venerable head to huzza, his silver hair streaming in the morning breeze, gave a livelier interest to the old man's address. Three wild cheers pealed along the ranks, the band struck up " God save the King," and the gallant grey showed himself not insensible to these demonstrations of military ardour, by rising proudly on his haunches, and neighing in unison with the cheers.

" So the game is again up," said the Captain of grenadiers, with a sigh, to the senior subaltern, as they walked home together.

" I am delighted," replied the Lieutenant, " I am at the head of the list, and my Company is now certain—What the devil! you look but dull on the business, Fred! what's the matter?"

" Zounds, man, I am only a month or two married, and to go away and leave—"

" Well, well, it will likely be another month or two before the route comes ; and for my part, if I was married, I should wish to hold my wife by the same tenure I hold my lodgings."

" Pshaw, hang your trifling ; I cannot, will not, leave poor Fanny—she would break her heart."

" Well, don't be soo gloomy about it ; you must remain behind, that's all."

B 2

" Eh ! what !" cried the Captain, evidently alarmed.

" And an exchange might be managed," continued his comforter. " Oh! I have it; you remember the day you dined with us, last week at the mess; old Captain O'Doud was there; he swore he would memorial to get from the Invalids into a marching regiment; he was good enough to say we were a jolly set, and probably might be induced—"

" Pshaw, damn O'Doud!"

" Why, as to O'Doud," continued the Lieutenant, drily, " I have no great hopes of him, for he was, what he good-naturedly termed, hazy, but what we imagined downright drunk, at the time ; and he's not just the thing for a marching regiment, as he wants a leg ;—but there's the man for your purpose, Major Mahaffy, who commands the Depôt here; he is anxious to get on active service ; his glass eye will not be any great objection; his charge is but a paltry concern of six honey-combed guns and rotten tumbrils, and as you have interest at the Horse-Guards, my life on it we will effect it."

" Why you intend to drive me mad—
O'Doud—Mahaffy;—but it is cruel to jest at
such a moment, O'Rourke; all is over, however, go I must—poor Fanny—the tears of the
sweetest eyes in Ulster cannot prevent it; I
must, as the song says, ' On with the knap-
sack and follow the drum.' "

" But are you not coming in to breakfast?"

" Why, no; weeping in the morning never
agreed with me, but I'll call after the first
volley of sighs is over."

O'Hara turned down to his lodgings, while
the Subaltern looked after him. " Stay at
home—no—not all the petticoats in Christen-
dom would keep him ; and, faith, that he's sorry
at leaving his wife, is not wonderful, for she's
an angel; God forbid she had thrown the temp-
tation of matrimony in my road, for I am but
a weak mortal—she fancied him too—he's a fine
dashing fellow; and game to the backbone ;
well, here I am with little, heaven knows, to
bother me ; the heart as light as the pocket,
and a Company across the water." O'Rourke
bolted up stairs, whistling a light jig, already
a Captain by anticipation.

The Captain's déjeuné was gloomy enough; he wished to convey the unexpected intelligence as gently as he could, and, as he reflected on the best manner of opening the unwelcome detail, so much care and abstraction was visible in his countenance as instantly to alarm his lady.

" Frederic, my dearest Frederic, has any thing given you pain ? You look disturbed— are you well ?''

" My love, the fact is, a flying report of a great military change has reached us this morning. I thought we were settled here for the Spring, and to spend the Summer at Harrowgate with your good uncle and sister ; I therefore dread that this will interfere with our arrangements, and as we soon expect a route for—"

He paused, finding himself hastening too rapidly to the denouement of the story. His wife fixed her dark eyes with a steady and penetrating glance on the agitated face of her husband :—

" So a change of quarters, I perceive, is certain ; come, come, O'Hara, tell me truth, the whole truth, are we ordered to the south of Ireland, among the wild men of the woods—or to England—or Scotland ?"

The Captain's features still preserved their gravity.

" Or are we to view the scenes of my uncle Toby's exploits in Flanders?"

The smile died on her lips, while her blanched cheeks betrayed the agitation she vainly endeavoured to conceal. O'Hara grew paler than his wife, and at last mustering all his courage, gradually communicated the Colonel's speech.

" To America! my God! is it possible?" as the tea-cup fell from her trembling fingers. O'Hara sprung from his chair.

" Sit down, Frederic—it is very foolish to be so frightened by a name. Well, when are we to go ?"

" We, dearest Fanny ; surely you could not think of crossing the Atlantic ; I had already determined to leave—."

" The regiment !" cried the lady, in a transport of delight.

The Captain's countenance flushed —" to

leave you comfortably settled at Bath with your sister."

"Leave me comfortably settled at Bath with my sister. Oh, Frederic! am I so cold-hearted as to be left comfortable at home, and the man of my heart exposed to death or danger? No, no, I am ready——go we will together; in health and happiness I will share your smiles, and in the hour of sorrow I will be near to comfort you. Yes, my adored husband, the tie that binds us together, death alone shall sever."

She threw her snowy arms around his neck, and as her tears fell upon his cheek, in the bitterness of the moment he cursed the hour which fated him to be a soldier.

Frederic O'Hara was born in the north of Ireland. In his earlier days, like a great proportion of his countrymen, he was handsome, gay, enterprising, and extravagant; but as he ripened into manhood, his native good sense corrected the errors of youthful indiscretion; judgment took the reins, and a strong and cultivated mind soon rendered him an estimable member of the community. The family of the

O'Hara's was aboriginal, and at no very distant period had been both rich and powerful; but, amidst the many fluctuations of property in the political convulsions, in these times so frequent, so much of their estates had been forfeited, that the inheritance of this haughty Sept had dwindled from a territory to a mountain district. On this stood a castellated building, erected on the ruins of the hold of the O'Haras, which, with many fortresses of this description, were dismantled during the Protectorate of Cromwell.

The family estate had been confided by the present possessor to the management of his uncle; and still remained under his faithful surveillance, when the unfortunate contest breaking out between the mother country and the colonies called the soldier into service. Never was there a harder struggle between love and glory; the latter, however, rose paramount, and the gallant Captain accompanied his regiment to the field.

Six months prior to the quarrel with the States, O'Hara married a lady named Moore; and although it seldom happens that love and interest go together in Ireland, yet in this case, there was an exception greatly in favour of the young soldier, as the object of his tenderest affections, unquestionably the reigning beauty of the fair circle in which she moved, was also seized in coheirship of a very considerable landed property. Fanny Moore was in her nineteenth year, and was more than handsome, possessed all the accomplishments of a finished education, with good sense and cheerful habits; she, with an only sister, was the issue of a second marriage. Her father's first wife was an English lady, with whom he got a considerable fortune; she had one child, a son. The mother was a complaining, ill-tempered invalid; and obedient to her humour, the child was educated, or rather suffered to remain uneducated at home, till he had gained his tenth year. At this period, Jonathan (as he was called after his maternal grandfather) lost his mamma, but, most unfortunately for him, she was not removed from this world until she had radically destroyed the temper and disposition of the heir: vain was all his father's endeavours to restore him to some sort of discipline—the boy was sulky and ungovernable; gentle and harsh measures were alternately tried, but, alas! with no good effect. By dint of sheer labour, that portion of reading and writing necessary for an Irish esquire was communicated to this refractory pupil; that is, the *quantum sufficit* for a receipt, or letter to a driver (bailiff) or dog-breaker. Jonathan had entered his thirteenth year, when his father, still in the prime of life, married the daughter of a respectable gentleman in the neighbourhood, whose pretensions to beauty and prudence were indisputable. But Jonathan differed in opinion from his father, and furiously resented the introduction of a step-mother. Mrs. Moore, amiable as lovely, endeavoured to win the stubborn brute by kindness and forbearance; the attempt always failed, and after a long distressing scene of family dissensions, protracted for seven years, the heir suddenly absconded from the house, and took up his abode with the Guager of the next village.

This last step mortally offended Moore; his instant return was commanded under the most solemn denunciations of eternal displeasure;

but the youth, under the tutelage of the officer
of customs, refused to obey the orders, declared
himself unawed by those threats of parental
vengeance, and in the course of a few days
completed his ruin by espousing the Guager's
daughter.   Moore was a determined man ; he
immediately made a will in favour of his wife
and her children, by which Jonathan was cut
off from every thing not in direct tail, and,
labouring to provide amply for the young favourites, he purchased properties, and erected
mills.   His industry was rewarded by a rapid
accumulation of fortune, and when in the midst
of this prosperous career, he fell a victim to his
humanity, dying of a typhus fever communicated during a visit to an afflicted tenant.

His relict, delicate in her constitution, and
deploring the death of her excellent husband,
found her health rapidly declining, and determined to reside for some years at Bath.   To
this she was especially induced by an accident
which happened to her younger daughter, at
first apparently so trifling as to be scarcely
noticed, but unfortunately in a short time terminating in total lameness—wretched health

accompanied this visitation, and the invalids were recommended to try a milder climate than their native one.

At Bath, the last seven years of Mrs Moore's life were devoted to the education and health of her children, when, to their inexpressible sorrow, she died suddenly, leaving them ample fortunes, and a richer inheritance derived from her own virtuous and honourable example. The orphan heiresses were now intrusted to the protection of their maternal uncle, a dignitary of the established church. He was an old bachelor, of a cheerful and hospitable disposition, and the Glebe-house was consequently frequented by all the respectable persons in the neighbourhood. Here, O'Hara, while visiting his small inheritance, was introduced to the Doctor's ward. The soldier was conquered at first sight, and immediately laid close siege to the lady. No very formidable resistance was offered, preliminaries having been satisfactorily discussed; a capitulation was concluded, and the worthy Prebendary surrendered his fair charge to the Captain of Grenadiers.

Poor Fanny idolized her young and handsome husband; and certainly, if honest Dryden says true, he did " deserve the fair." The orders of readiness for the regiment were consequently to her distracting. She, however, hesitated not; and contrary to the wishes of her husband and relatives, and heedless of her own situation, then evidently unfitted for sharing fatigue and danger, she instantly determined to accompany him to the scene of action. They embarked at Cork in the beginning of April, and landed in Boston Bay in the latter end of May, 1775.

It may not be unnecessary to take a short retrospective view of the affairs of this country for some years prior to the time of O'Hara's visit. The home administration of American affairs, from its ruinous policy, had been long alarming. In positive infringement of colonial charters, an attempt was made by the Court of St. James, to draw a direct revenue to the treasury of Great Britain, by the introduction of stamped paper. This first infringement on their rights met, of course, with a warm resistance from the Americans; and when the Ministry found it necessary to repeal this obnoxious impost, they endeavoured, by indirect taxation, to place a portion of the heavy burden at home on the shoulders of the Colonists abroad. The attempt was too apparent in its object not to be easily discovered, and steadily rejected. Here, then, the business should have been abandoned; but following up an unsatisfactory and vacillating policy, one grievance was removed only to be replaced by another—oppression produced resistance, and the Americans solemnly combined against the consumption of any taxable article of British merchandise. The teas from the East India House were returned unlanded to the Company who shipped them; or when a small quantity found its way on shore, it was suffered to rot unsold in the vaults of Charleston. In Boston no middle course was adopted, for the mob boarded the vessel which brought this obnoxious cargo and committed its contents to the waves.

At this time perhaps an abandonment on the part of Ministers, of measures, unwise as they were unjust, might have been attended with eminent success : but they had passed the Rubicon, and nothing kind, nothing conciliatory

issued from the Cabinet; on the contrary, harsh
and tyrannical proceedings were resorted to;
the malecontents were branded as insurgents,
and their most popular leaders proscribed.
The inhabitants of Boston, in particular, were
treated with unexampled severity; for, by the
passing of a cruel law, entitled "The Boston
Port Bill," the harbour was closed, and consequently their trade utterly destroyed.

The Colonists thus finding themselves marked
out as victims of unrelenting persecution, determined not to be coldly submissive. In public and in private, a dangerous discussion of
freedom and independence became universal—
from the press flowed torrents of remonstrance
and reproach—pageants representing the death
and resuscitation of liberty were exhibited in
the public streets—persons holding obnoxious
places under the government were executed in
effigy—the guards insulted at their posts, and
the carriage of the governor burnt beneath the
guns of Fort William; till at last the sword, so
long suspended by a hair, fell—it was drawn
in the cause of freedom, and red indeed was the
blade before it could be sheathed again.

The bad terms on which the inhabitants and the military were, rendered a residence in Boston, as may be well imagined, not very desirable. This town had always been the focus of the revolution, and the first shot fired in the infancy of resistance was here discharged from the guard-house of the 29th Regiment.— The mob and the soldiery had been continually embroiled—at this moment martial law prevented any thing like commotion in the streets; but those feelings which circumstances rendered it prudent to conceal, were becoming more hostile and inveterate. From the factious temper of the lower classes, and the avowed revolutionary principles of the more respectable, all intercourse had long ceased to subsist between the military and the citizens; each party felt uncomfortable in the other's presence, this viewing that with fear, and the other in return looking on them with distrust. In short, all within Boston was repulsive and unfriendly—all without gloomy and portentous.

Before the arrival of the forty-seventh regiment in America, actual hostilities had commenced. General Gage at that time com-

manded in Boston, and understanding that the
village of Concord, about twenty miles distant
from the city, had been made a depôt for the
arms and stores of the insurgent colonists, it
was deemed advisable by him to surprise it.
Notwithstanding the precautionary measures
adopted by the General, the advance of the
royalists was discovered, and they found the
militia and colonial troops in readiness to oppose them. The British, however, succeeded
with great difficulty in effecting the desired
object, by destroying the stores of the republicans; but on their return they were fiercely
and incessantly pursued, and although relieved
by a strong detachment of infantry with two
field-pieces, under the command of Lord Percy,
they suffered dreadfully on their retreat, until
completely exhausted, they halted on the height
of Bunker's Hill. On that day of excessive
fatigue, the royal army had marched upwards
of forty miles, exposed at every step of the retreat to the deadly fire of the American riflemen. Their loss in killed alone was estimated
at two hundred men.

CHAPTER II.

Duke.—And what's her history ?
Viola.—A blank, my lord.
Twelfth Night.

THE consequences of the affair at Lexington (as it was called) were truly important. The Americans, elated by victory, and confident of ultimate success, prepared for an energetic resistance, while the opinion generally entertained in England of the inefficacy of the colonial forces was discovered to have been miserably incorrect; and the grenadier cap, so imposing to the inexperienced soldier in its appearance, returned from the plains of Concord, robbed of its fancied terrors.

The alarm felt at Boston was general. The arrival, however, of large reinforcements from Ireland, tended in a great measure to remove it. The flank companies of the respective regiments were landed without delay, and Captain O'Hara and his lady accommodated with lodgings in the town.

The Captain soon arranged a tolerably comfortable establishment; an elderly man and woman, who had resided for many years with his deceased father, accompanied him. A grenadier, a native of the county of Tipperary, attended his horses and the out-door work, and a very handsome young English girl, whom Mr. Mahony, the aforesaid grenadier, had persuaded, during the " piping-time of peace," to elope with him, served the lady in the capacity of waiting-maid.

The residence selected by the Captain's wife, for the time she might remain in Boston, was situated at the extremity of the city, commanding, in the distance, a fine view of a rich and wooded country, indented by a spacious bay. The British fleet were anchored beneath the town, and the heights of Bunker's Hill occupied and closed the left of the prospect. The more immediate objects which met the eye were very dissimilar. The windows of the Captain's rooms opened on a small enclosure,

in which that class of people, called Quakers,
interred their departed friends. It was sym-
bolical of their lives,—simple, retired, and
unimposing. None disturbed its green alleys
with a footstep, save the relatives of its peaceful occupiers. The turf was raised into
mounds in lines of striking regularity; each
grassy hillock denoting, that those who had
once lived, there slept " the sleep that knows
no breaking." At one end of the green, a
plain wooden building was erected; its low-
liness and retirement happily according with
the devotions of a meek and broken spirit:
close hedges, supported by a lofty row of pop-
lars, seemed to protect the dead from the
living. One wicket opened in the leafy wall;
it was low and narrow, for those who entered
it were lowly. Here, indeed, might it be said,
that " the wicked ceased from troubling, and
the weary were at rest." But a few paces
from this peaceful cemetery, an object of a
very opposite description appeared: it was a
strong bastion, which, from commanding the
eastern angle of the works, had been fortified
with great care. Guns, of the largest calibre,

were pointed from the embrasures ; an English
ensign, raised on an elevated flag-staff, floated
gaily in the centre of the esplanade ; sentry-
boxes were placed at either extremity ; numerous piles of shot were built between the
cannon, while a deep ditch, the outer side
defended by a chevaux-de-frise, and the inner
edge stockaded, secured the battery from any
hostile approach.

The grave, the closing scene of the drama
of human life, is seldom regarded with insen-
sibility. Its loneliness is imposing, and it steals
imperceptibly on the senses, till they slumber in placid forgetfulness, and the bustle
of the world, its joys and sorrows, its business and pleasures, are for a time forgotten. No spot could have been more fa-
vourably chosen to excite such feelings than
the burying-ground of the Friends of Boston. But if the eye wandered for a moment from the spot it rested on, the illusion
ceased, the dream was dissolved, and war,
with its horrible realities, recalled the senses
to perception.

It was the month of June. The day had

been sultry, but the evening was mild and lovely. Mrs. O'Hara was seated at an open window ; her husband sketching with his pencil from a collection of American scenery ; the door of the apartment unclosed, and Captain Edwards of the 38th Regiment, a distant relative and favourite companion of O'Hara, entered. Edwards was in the bloom of life ; his manners most insinuating, his conversation lively, his honour unsullied. He had one foible,—call it rather a crime,—he was always in love, and always changing his mistress. So strong had this habit increased, (for it was one,) that although betrothed to a lovely girl, of high family and splendid fortune, in England, and to whom, on his return, he was to be united, yet he could not meet a female with disengaged affections, without endeavouring to win them. Too frequently he succeeded, and if he failed, it was to him a matter of profound indifference. Such was the defect of otherwise a first-rate character. In friendship faithful as in love inconstant; the soldier of chivalry, nothing was too desperate for his daring courage to attempt, and the humanity and

kindness of his disposition had made him the
idol of his regiment.   He had been two years
in America, and, in an encounter with a party
of hostile Indians, had most eminently distinguished himself : in this affair he was severely
wounded, but recovered to receive the thanks
of his commanding officer, and the light company of the 38th Regiment.

Edwards was extremely attached to O'Hara,
and from the mutual pleasure each felt in the
other's society, a large portion of their time
was generally passed together : one circumstance in his friend's conduct appeared unaccountable to O'Hara.   Since his return to
Boston, his brother-officers had remarked that
Edwards had been at times much depressed,
but the cause was studiously concealed, and
no entreaty could induce him to divulge it,
even to those who had hitherto possessed his
unbounded confidence.   " I know not," said
he, as he seated himself, " how to account for
the unusual dulness of my spirits to-day.   I
have been writing to England to——," he smiled,
and paused,—" and, although I have always
felt that writing or receiving letters exhila-

rated my sober spirits, yet in this case it has lost its effect. To *my* taste the wine was sour, though all the others praised it; and the laugh which echoed from the table was loud and unharmonious to me alone. I have come," continued he, smiling, " where I shall be relieved ; for you, Mrs. O'Hara, and that light-hearted Irishman, are always cheerful: Ha! the wine has recovered its flavour."

" That wine will improve in the next bottle wonderfully," replied O'Hara; " but, see, for a wonder, a living creature enters that dismal burying-place." The object of his attention was carefully securing the little gate which had admitted him. He was provided with a spade and shovel, and advanced to the upper end of the green: his appearance was grave and melancholy, and indicated that he had nearly reached the longest span of human existence. He was, probably, eighty years old, and yet, from the temperance of his youth, his step was firm and manly. Stopping beneath the window where O'Hara stood, he viewed the spot for a few moments, took off his plain, brown coat, folded and placed it on the adjacent hillock, and then steadily commenced his labour.

" It is late in the evening to begin to work," said O'Hara.

" Even so," replied the old man.

" For whom are you making that grave ?"

" For a maiden who is gathered to her fathers."

" Was the woman who is dead young?" said Edwards.

" The damsel is not dead, but sleepeth; she was seventeen years born."

" So young," exclaimed Edwards, " it is a pity that one in the spring of life should be so prematurely hurried to the tomb."

" That is the end of all men, and the living should lay it to heart," said the grave-digger, as he looked steadily at Edwards.

" Pray," said Mrs. O'Hara, " what did the young woman die of ?"

" Grief," replied the old man.

" Good heavens !" said Edwards, " what caused it ?"

The senior again raised his eyes from the ground, and resting a look of strong expression on the countenance of the inquirer, replied with great emotion, "" One habited as thou art caused her death."

Edwards coloured, and retired from the window.

The interest of the listeners was now powerfully awakened, and O'Hara, not perceiving the embarrassment of his friend, pursued his inquiries with eagerness. The old man slowly replied to his numerous interrogatories, until the melancholy story was told.

It appeared, that the young woman's family resided in the back lands, three hundred miles from Boston, and possessed a rich and extensive plantation. She was the only daughter of her parents, who had, however, several sons. A small British post established in the vicinity of the farm, had been surprised during a dark and stormy night by a hostile band of Indians. They made a desperate assault on the little garrison, but, by the gallantry of the young officer who commanded, were eventually beaten off: he was, however, dangerously wounded.

O'Hara was startled by a low groan, and,

on turning about, perceived Edwards was
deeply affected. He leaned against the 'l
behind him, with his face buried in his 's;
while, in the simple language of his ---t, the
old man continued his relation.

" They bore him in the morning to the house
where Rachel sojourned with her kindred.
Blood flowed from his breast, and the hand of
death seemed to be hard upon him. Oil was
poured into his wounds, and he lay upon the
softest bed. She, who is now at rest, was lovely
to the eye, and the stranger had a stately form.
Often did the damsel sit by his side, and minister to his wants, for her brethren and kindred laboured daily in the fields. The warrior
told the maiden of his love, and entreated her
to leave the house of her fathers, and flee with
him from the fold of the faithful. Long did
she refuse ; but, at last, consented to become
his spouse. One day, he who served him
brought a letter, saying, ' He who command-
eth thy band hath written.' He was yet weak,
and he besought the damsel to read to him
what was therein contained. She consented,
and read. The letter was from his betrothed

wnte. ɪɪer senses fled, and she swooned away;
b when she revived, she hastened from his
pv. . ce, and never saw him more! Shame
struck him to the quick,—he arose and left the
house, and went I know not whither. Rachel wept in her chamber, but her tears were
in secret; she pined, and none knew where-
fore. She smiled not by day, neither in the
night season did she slumber. Her parents,
sorrowing, arose and carried her hither, that
those skilled in medicine might minister to her
cure; but it was in vain! She departed the
night before last, praying while her breath
remained for the Gentile youth who had deceived her."

Ere the little narrative had concluded, Edwards, uttering a cry of horror, rushed from
the room.

The scene was melancholy!—Mrs. O'Hara
wept over the untimely fate of poor Rachel
with unaffected sorrow. In a short time after,
approaching footsteps were heard. It was the
funeral. A number of serious-looking people,
of both sexes, advanced, carrying a simple bier,
on which a plain, unornamented coffin rested.

It was now twilight, and objects could not be seen with distinctness. Low and smothered sobs were heard, indicating that the mourners were endeavouring to conceal the grief they could not conquer. As the grave gradually filled up, the lament of Rachel's brothers grew more difficult to stifle ; till at length the melancholy business was completed, and the attendants departed silently. One, an elderly person, and probably her father, lingered for a few moments behind the others, apparently engaged in mental devotion. He bowed his head with deep humility, and pronouncing in a low but steady voice, " He gave, and He hath taken away," retired, and the gate was fastened.

Mrs. O'Hara daily expected to be confined ; and every young female at that period must be apprehensive for her safety : her character was naturally of a timid cast, and the fate of the youthful Quakeress had depressed her spirits. " I feel," she said, as she hid her tearful cheek in her husband's bosom, " that it is great cruelty to you to yield thus to despondency—I cannot avoid it, for something whispers me that this ominous country will be fatal to our happiness. *You*, O'Hara, will unnecessarily expose yourself,—your forwardness and striking figure will fatally distinguish you, and you will fall by the rifle of some nameless republican. The fears I entertain for myself are small, for I trust that God will support me in my approaching trial; should it be otherwise ordained,—and, Heaven pardon me, I would be most unwilling to part from my beloved Frederic,—lay me beside poor Rachel, fly from this devoted country, and in the peaceful scenes we quitted, sometimes remember the woman who adored you."

O'Hara, in great agitation, caught her to his bosom: "Oh! Fanny! talk not in such melancholy words—all will yet be well, and we shall be happy; on your account, I would act every part but the coward's—but now to draw back, to leave my regiment on service, and return ingloriously to degrading obscurity —no, the name of O'Hara was never coupled with reproach, and I will not be the first to stain it."

"Frederic, I would not ask you; my hus-

band must be still a gentleman and a soldier;
but if we live to return once more to dear
Ireland, will you abandon this terrible profession? Your property suffers by the absence of its master; for my sake, for the sake
of your expected infant, leave, when you can
with honour, a profession which destroys the
happiness of your wife, and militates against
the future fortunes of your offspring."——He
kissed fondly the tears from her cheek, "Who
could withstand your smiles? but your tears
are unanswerable. Yes,—I agree; I will consent to your wishes, but you must wait till I
can do it as an O'Hara ought—but, poor
Edwards, my erring, unfortunate kinsman,
from my heart I pity him. I know his hasty
disposition might prompt him to some act of
rashness. I must go and stay with him for a
short time, and at supper, let my darling
Fanny be once more cheerful." The Captain
affectionately kissed his smiling wife, and left
her apartment to seek that of his repentant
friend.

CHAPTER III.

'Tis done! 'tis done! that fatal blow
  Has stretch'd him on the bloody plain;
He strives to rise,—brave Musgrave, no;
  Thence never shalt thou rise again.

Lay of the Last Minstrel.

O'HARA reached the lodgings of his country-man, and cautiously knocking at the door, was admitted by the servant, who appeared in considerable alarm; recognising with visible pleasure his master's companion, he proceeded to inform him that the Captain, after being absent for a short time after dinner, had returned completely out of his senses. For the first time in his life he had treated him with great harshness; and on his hesitating to leave him in the distracted state in which he seemed to be, furiously commanded his absence, in a tone which precluded any refusal. For some time he had continued in considerable agitation of mind, pacing the chamber with rapid and unequal steps : latterly he appeared more composed, and the servant imagined that he had perhaps thrown himself on the bed. O'Hara gently ascended the stairs, and tapped at the door ; an angry voice from within demanded who knocked, but on ascertaining that his kinsman was there, desired him to enter. He was leaning against the chimney-piece, his eyes wild and wandering, his look unsettled, seemingly abandoning himself to despair. O'Hara attempted in vain to offer some consolation to the sufferer, but was hastily interrupted,— "Would you have believed it, had not your own ears listened to the tale, that Henry Edwards was the gallant honourable gentleman he is ? Bleeding, fainting, expiring, he was carried to the house of innocence,—but peace and happiness left that dwelling when the traitor entered. He was admitted, for humanity abode there ; every kindness was lavished on him ; an angel, yes, a pure, artless, unsuspicious angel, nursed him tenderly ; he recovered, and could he but be grateful ? Oh, yes, yes, he flat-

tered, he sighed, he swore that he passionately
loved her. She, the child of nature, believed
him ; she consented to give up home, kindred,
religion. And when he had effected all this,
for more the villain could not effect, he deserted her, deceived her, murdered her"———
and an hysteric sob concluded a speech delivered with all the frantic enunciation of a
maniac. The last burst of passion, however,
exhausted his strength, and sinking down on a
chair beside him, O'Hara saw with delight
tears falling fast upon the floor : as he expected, the poignancy of his distress was relieved, and with calmness, but in terms of the
most heartfelt sorrow, he lamented the fate of
the girl to whom he declared he had been tenderly attached. His friend remained for a considerable time, and then rose to depart ; Edwards having promised that he would retire to
bed, and endeavour to compose himself to
sleep.

It was late when the Captain retired to his
lodgings ; the road leading to his home was
totally deserted, the inhabitants having long
since closed their houses for the night. Now

and then some lonely sentinel at a corner challenged and received the countersign; this was common to every garrison-town, and was apparently but a part of military form. Although Boston was filled with British soldiery, their discipline prevented tumult or confusion. At times, through the stillness of the night, the " All's well " from the shipping moored under cover of the cannon of the town, was heard, mellowed by the distance; but it was a sound rather calculated to allay than excite alarm. It was known that a large body of Americans was encamped in the neighbourhood, but that they should commence a course of active operations was by no means to be apprehended, and the earlier part of the night of the 16th of June passed in uninterrupted tranquillity.

Mr. and Mrs. O'Hara had been late in retiring to their chamber; interested in the events of the preceding evening, his sleep was restless and disturbed; a bugle, but scarcely audible, seemed to sound; he started, and all was quiet. He lay listening in anxious suspense, and the bugle sounded distinctly. He arose in silence, fearing the slumbers of his lady should be broken, and was hurrying on his uniform, when a signal gun from the shipping was discharged. Mrs. O'Hara was fearfully awakened, and as her husband endeavoured to calm her alarm, the drums beat ; a knocking at the door was heard, and the voice of Edwards demanded admission. The Captain hastened to the outer room to receive him, and was astonished to see a covered caravan, drawn up beneath the window. " Rise quickly, O'Hara, the Americans possess the hill ; the battery behind your house will open in a few minutes,—my lodgings are retired,—remove Mrs. O'Hara instantly to them." The lady and her servants were hastily put in motion, and before the eastern bastion had sufficient light to train its cannon upon the enemy's works, Mrs. O'Hara was landed in safety in the abode of her husband's friend.

As the caravan proceeded, Edwards addressed his companion,—" After you left me, I sat down to write ; I finished what I was engaged in, and determined to visit the place where my lost Rachel is interred. I succeeded in passing the enclosure, and seated myself on the turf which covers her remains. I had not been long there before I imagined that I heard the distant report of a musket; I started up, and was hastening to the battery to ask whether the sentinel had also heard it, when the bugle sounded; that caravan was passing at the moment, I stopped the unwilling driver, and aware that your house was in a trouble-some neighbourhood, I thought Mrs. O'Hara would be more remote from the firing in my lodgings. We shall be shortly engaged: in a private drawer of my writing-desk a sealed paper is deposited; these stubborn fellows have got possession of a strong eminence, it may be difficult to dislodge them; I will be in the scramble. Should I fall, open the little memorial, and endeavour to carry its wishes into effect. But we are at the door. Come, my dear Mrs. O'Hara, these unmannerly guns are noisy, but fear nothing, here you are in security." Leading the way to his apart-ments, he welcomed his fair guest, and telling her he would go to learn the extent of the general alarm, he left her, as we shall take the liberty of doing for a time, in peaceable possession of her friendly quarters.

The town of Boston is beautifully situated; it is seated on a peninsula, divided from Charleston by a river, and commanded on the eastern side by the strong eminence of Bunker's-Hill. On the night above mentioned, the Americans had taken possession of those heights, and labouring with astonishing silence, threw up before the morning dawned a line of works extending half a mile across the summit of the ridge. When discovered, a heavy fire was opened on the working parties, from the guns of the men-of-war and the batteries of the city; but apparently undisturbed by the cannonade, by noon they completed their lines. To dislodge them from this strong position was now as difficult as it was necessary, and a body of troops were ordered on that service. Twenty flank companies, supported by the 5th, 38th, 43d, 47th, and 52d regiments, a battalion of marines, and a light brigade of artillery, were formed at the foot of this formidable eminence. General Howe with the grenadiers advanced

against the lines, while General Pigot with
the light infantry was directed to carry a
redoubt which flanked the left of the enemy.
The British troops advanced up the hill with
fearless intrepidity, but on approaching the
entrenchments the republican fire opened with
such fatal precision, that the best soldiers in
Europe were checked, wavered, and broken.
The execution of the rifle was terrible ; and
the artillery, worked with rapidity and effect,
poured upon the gallant assailants a deadly
torrent of grape, and canister shot. General
Howe, whose approved bravery was most
conspicuous at the trying moment, rushed into
the hottest of the fire. Officers and men fell
in heaps around him ; " surrounded by the
dying and the dead," he preserved his wonted
composure, rallying the remains of the grenadiers who had led the attack, pointed with his
sword to the breast-work, and cheered them
to a fresh essay.

O'Hara's company had twice advanced, and
their leader armed with the musket and bayonet of a fallen soldier, was seen conspicuously
at their head. They had been a second time

beaten back, leaving half their number on the
" glacis" of the entrenchment. At this critical moment, when the day was all but lost,
General Clinton arrived from Boston. The
British once more were formed, and again
pressed forward to the trenches. O'Hara and
the grenadiers a third time headed the storm-
ing party with all the desperate valour of his
country. He entered the ditch, followed by
his men, and British and American engaged
hand to hand. General Warren, who commanded the American right, had throughout
this arduous conflict displayed the greatest
bravery ; he rallied his raw soldiery, and
rushing to the front, endeavoured sword in
hand to expel the intruders. Warren and
O'Hara met ; the young American discharged
a pistol at the Captain of grenadiers, while
O'Hara, springing forward, plunged his bayonet into the breast of his gallant adversary.
Dismayed by his fall, the Republicans gave
way, and the entire of the right division were
soon across the ditch. On the left, the redoubt which had strengthened that part of the
works had foiled General Pigot in the repeated

attempts which he had made to possess it, but seizing on the diversion made in his favour by the success of the British right, he succeeded by a well-timed and vigorous effort in turning the flank of the American defences. The Royalists instantly occupied the hardly contested heights, and their brave opponents, after an heroic resistance, retreated over the hill with all the steadiness of a veteran army.

The operations of the English forces did not terminate with the defeat of the Republicans. The town of Charleston had annoyed them during the day, by a constant teazing fire, and, in revenge, it was devoted to the flames. Consisting of nearly five hundred wooden houses, and these being fired in many places at the same moment, the conflagration was indeed awful. The lofty spire of the meeting-house, constructed of the pitch-pine tree, shot a brilliant column of fire to an immense height, and exhibited to the numerous lookers-on, who had viewed the engagement from the walls of Boston, a spectacle not inferior in horror even to the field of battle,—a city sheeted in one unbroken mass of flames.

The feelings of O'Hara, as he gazed on the surrounding objects, were indescribable. The trenches, on the bank of which he stood, were filled with dead and wounded republicans ; people of similar manners, speaking the same language, and closely related by descent, could not, in this scene of destruction, be regarded without a lively sympathy. Those of the Americans who had fallen at any distance were scarcely to be discovered from the earth in which they rested. Nothing on these self-taught soldiers was intended to strike the eye. Their blue dresses and dark rifles were without ornament. All was plain, but all was effective. Far differently appeared the British Grenadiers. Arrayed in uniforms profusely decorated, burthened with showy and useless accoutrements, with polished arms, belts, and breast-plates ; all too well calculated to bestow a melancholy distinction on the wearer, and make him a more marked object for the rifleman.

O'Hara sickened as he looked down the hill. It was, indeed, a melancholy sight. Heaps of corses lay as if regularly strewn in

front of the breast-work, and indicated with
what unflinching courage the British had advanced to the assault. The gay habiliments of
the fallen officers gave to the field of death a
gloomier contrast. Caps and feathers, mus-
kets and drums, as they had dropped from the
relaxing grasp of their possessors, were loosely
scattered about ; while, as if to crown the
horror of the whole, the light which glanced
upon the scene of slaughter was reddened by
the flames of Charleston. O'Hara was nearly
exhausted : he had received several slight
wounds which were bleeding freely. A gun,
which the retreating Americans had disabled,
to prevent it from being turned on their rear,
was beside him, and resting against it, he endeavoured to bind up his wounds, when his
attention was roused by the voice of a soldier,
whose tones were familiar to his ear, entreating the assistance of a comrade. The fellow
had been wounded in the fleshy part of the
thigh, and was (to make use of his own term)
striving to " hough out the ball." The assistance which he had solicited was kindly,
but clumsily, administered by a Scotch drum-

mer, and during an awkward operation, Mahony (for it was O'Hara's servant) bore it with unmoved stoicism. "It's out, at last, sweet Jasus be praised," exclaimed the attendant, "and may-be I won't be easier with it in my pocket than if it was in my leg, if I felt as sore since Doctor Maginty (the devil's luck to him!) pulled out the wrong tooth instead of the right one. God bless you, Sandy dear,— but you done it neatly. Ogh, Captain, the blood's runnin down your jacket : take a drop, it's only wine, for you know I am booked agin spirits till Lammas, barrin what's given me out of your own hand, or Serjeant Grady's; and if I never drink till the Serjeant gives it to me, well as I liked him, by my soul, I would not like to see him now that he's dead, for he's kilt out and out."

"Poor fellow," said O'Hara, "he was a noble soldier."

"And as clane a made man," said Mahony, "as ever went into a field."

"Did you see him fall?" asked the drummer.

"Fall!" echoed the grenadier, "wasn't I beside him, man. 'Serjeant,' says I, 'will

we ever get over that damn'd shough?'   ' Arrah, what will hinder us ?' says he.   ' Heads
up, boys, and at them again.'   With that, the
ball hit him, and down he went.   I was stopping to lift him, but he beckoned me off.
' Forward,' says he, ' my darlings, for I'm
done for : the blessings of the Almighty attend
yees, and my curse and the devil's pursue the
first man that shows the number of his knap-
sack.'   He strove to shout, but that was too
much for him, over he went on his face, and
died like a rael haro."

The eulogy on the departed Serjeant
was interrupted by a heavy sigh.   Mahony
looked over his shoulder with great indifference, and continued—

" It's the gentleman your honour jagged
with the bayonet : I thought it was all over
with him.   Hould his head up, Sandy, and I'll
give him a drop to keep the life in him."

" Poor boy," said the Hibernian, as he unbuttoned a jacket, handsomely but plainly or-
namented.   " Here's a love-token hid in his
breast."

The dying American seemed to apprehend
the loss of the miniature, probably the portrait

of his mistress, and made a feeble effort to retain it. His wishes were understood by the speaker.

" Is it me take it ? Oh no ! you have been tenderly and genteelly reared ; and as to your keep-sake, no one shall titch it, and me by. But, hauld up," continued he, in a tone of kind encouragement, " they'll lift us soon, and we'll go together to the hospital. Af there's a squeeze, which I allow there will, you and I can have a shake down together. You fought hard, and the devil take them that would lave you. You got a sore prod, my jewel, but it's a comfort to know that it was a rael gentleman that gave you it."

Warren's head rested on O'Hara's knee, and he appeared to recognise him as the officer who had wounded him. He gently took the supporting hand, and pressed it feebly to his breast. His eyelids closed,—the fingers gra- dually relaxed their pressure,—and a low groan, accompanied by a convulsive motion of the limbs, announced that Warren ceased to live.

This last scene was too much for the rival

soldier. Agitated by the tenderest solicitude, faint with fatigue and loss of blood, and quite unable to support himself, he leaned over the corse of the fallen American. Warren had only entered into his twenty-third year, and added to a face, perhaps too feminine in its beauty, a figure of faultless symmetry. The wound in his breast had bled profusely, and the locket which he seemed to value so dearly glittered in a dark halo of blood.

Love did not want its association in the ideas of O'Hara, and, as he thought on the forlorn situation of his wife, he groaned in an agony of distress. General Howe at the moment rode up,—sprang from his horse, and embracing him, noticed his excessive agitation, and kindly entreated to know the cause.

Mahony, who had been looking at his master with great anxiety, perceiving that he was unable to reply, instantly exclaimed,—

" Your honour sees that he is wounded, and, besides, he's frettin about her Ladyship; for when me and the master marched, her Honour's time was in, and they allowed she was going to take labour. Och ! it's I would have been home to tell her, that the Captain was alive and merry, only the devil a leg I could put before the other."

To summon an orderly with a steady horse—to place O'Hara on his back, and offer the warmest wishes for his lady's safety, was all the work of an instant. The Captain rode quietly down the hill. The General gallopped forward to recall the advance, and Pat Mahony, after commending his master and mistress to the especial care of Heaven, seated himself beside the body of the Republican Commander.

CHAPTER IV.

No useless coffin enclosed his breast,
  Not in sheet or in shroud we bound him ;
He lay like a warrior taking his rest,
  With his martial cloak around him.

Wolfe.

THOUSANDS were spectators of the engagement from the eminences of Boston, and its en-
virons; and as O'Hara advanced into the town,
his appearance attracted the undivided attention
of the lookers on. The soldiers who were off
duty, and citizens in detached groups, still occupied the walls from whence they had gazed
on the field of battle, with equal anxiety, but
dissimilar feelings.

The soldier, as he viewed the fluctuations of
the conflict, trembled for the safety and honour
of his companions in arms; and when victory
and the hill was theirs, his triumph broke out
in wild and unrestrained exultation : while the

citizen, with keener sensibility, almost sank
beneath the blow which threatened to crush, in
its infant struggle for independence, the future
liberties of a great and growing country. The
Royalist with delight, the Republican with sorrow and devotion, still turned their eyes on the
spot where the first martyrs of American freedom bled—though they failed to conquer;
while O'Hara, cheered by the one, and coldly
stared at by the other, interrogated by a multitude, to whose opposite questions it was impossible to reply, at last found his further progress barred by a brigade of soldiers' wives,
who seemed obstinate in their determination to
dispute the passage. In a state of great ex-
haustion, he was badly conditioned to free himself from this troublesome group, when his old
servant, with heartfelt joy pictured in his
countenance, rushed stoutly through the surrounding amazons, and led off the object of
their curiosity. The Captain was anticipated
in his inquiry for his lady, and listened with
rapturous delight to the account of her safety,
and the birth of an heir.

" She had a fine time, considering; and now

that his honour was returned with the life in
him, all would be well."

He shortly arrived at his friend's apartments
—his servant assisted him to dismount; and,
while the news of his safe return was cautiously
conveyed to the invalid, his wounds were examined, and being found but trifling, were
dressed by the Physician, who fortunately had
not left the house; and soon the tears of as
brave a soldier as any who bled on the heights
of Bunker's-Hill, fell in more than womanly
affection on the cheek of his now happy wife.

There were few that day in Boston who did
not share in the general distress. The Americans apprehended that the British troops would
follow up their victory, and push forward without delay to their head-quarters at Cambridge;
and probably an advance at this critical period
would have fatally decided the cause of the
Revolution—nothing could have saved their
discomfitted army from total dispersion; while,
with revived confidence, those who were well
affected to the existing Government, would
have been animated to have seconded them by
their co-operation. But the loss of the victors

had been too severe to warrant their commencing an active course of annoyance with any prospect of success; and accordingly they advanced no farther than the field of battle, where they threw up additional works for their security. The Provincial Forces halted on Prospect-Hill, occupying an entrenched position in their front, both parties carefully guarding against an attack, which each well knew they were but badly prepared to oppose.

With rest and refreshment, O'Hara's strength was wonderfully recruited; and now free from any apprehensions for his lady's or his own safety, he felt anxiously for that of his companions. Edwards principally engrossed his attention; and, as several hours had elapsed since the engagement terminated, and no tidings of his friend, although repeatedly sought for, had yet arrived, he determined, with the assistance of his servant, to proceed to his former residence, whither he had ordered Mahony to be carried as soon as the wounded were brought in. On the way, he found the fears he entertained for Edward's safety confirmed, as he was informed he had been severely wounded, and

agreeably to his particular directions, carried
to the house of O'Hara. On arriving at the
door, he entered with so much silence, that for
some moments he was an unobserved spectator
of what was passing in the room. Pat Mahony,
stretched on a mattress in a corner, was observing with apparent solicitude, the striking group
which occupied the centre of the apartment.
The light was sad and sombre—the windows
were blinded, with the exception of that before
which Edwards, lying on a couch, was supported by a soldier seated behind him; the
Regimental Surgeon, examining a wound in his
breast on one side, and a grave, heart-broken
looking man kneeling on the other, with one
of the patient's hands clasped between his
own; his face was deadly pale, and the blood,
which a bandage could not staunch, was trick-
ling from a sabre cut in his forehead. O'Hara
came forward, and Edwards instantly recognised him with an exclamation of joy, and
placing his arm around his friend's neck, kissed
him with fervent affection. The Surgeon, raising his head, glanced his eye at O'Hara, and
fatally that glance told that Edwards's fate in

this world was decided. Tears falling down the rugged cheeks of the supporting soldier, and Mahony's frequent sobs, indicated that they too had remarked that ominous look.

None but the sufferer himself was unmoved, and with a voice of amazing steadiness, he smilingly, but feebly, addressed O'Hara:—

" From my heart I congratulate you. What was my pride when lying on the field, I heard the shout of ' Ireland for ever!—O'Hara and victory!' And your wife and the little stranger, too—I have heard all, but have neither strength nor words to say how happy I wish them. Hold—do not close that window—it was my only prayer to be carried here, and I can now die without a wish ungratified."

A sun-beam fell partially on the green, and rested for a moment on Rachel's grave. The dying soldier remarked it, and exclaimed with wild enthusiasm—" Yes, blessed beam, if you light upon that spot to-morrow, I shall be there also!"

His extremities were now cold, and he complained that he felt chilly, and carelessly asked how long he might still linger? The Surgeon, to whom the question was addressed, turned his head hastily aside to conceal excessive agitation. " I read my answer," said Edwards, coolly, " and my last route is come—but my peace is made—with Rachel I sleep to-night, and none can sever the union of the dead ; though not in life, yet in death I shall be thine, Rachel !"

The old man burst into a flood of tears, as he said mournfully, " Thou mayest go to her, but she shall never come to thee ;" and stooping down, affectionately kissed him.

Edwards asked for wine, and having with difficulty swallowed a glass-full, he continued —" I feel I have not many minutes to live ; hear me, Frederic—you have a son, will you, in remembrance of your deceased kinsman, call him Henry Edwards ?" O'Hara pressed his hand in token of the compliance to which his lips could not give utterance. " What I esteem most valuable, I leave him—my sword— it was my father's—stainless it descended to me, and the son of O'Hara will never disgrace a gallant weapon. When I am breathless, place me in the earth as I now lie, coffinless. His uniform should ever be a soldier's winding-sheet.

Lay me close to Rachel—let not even a turf fall between me and my bride. I wish the remnant of my own company to carry me to the grave, and if they think I merited them, let them pay me the last honours of a soldier. I am dying: tell your wife I sent her my last love; and when your son asks who was Henry Edwards, tell him he was born a soldier, and that he died one. Can you see Bunker's-Hill, O'Hara? Bring me closer to the window—but no, it is useless. It was a noble battle for America; and those who can fight so well for freedom, deserve it. Who closed that window? 'Tis only a mist shading my sight. I am going fast. God bless—"

The contest was over, the sufferer at rest—an internal hæmorrhage had stopped the play of the lungs suddenly, and with his glassy eye still strained on the grave of his beloved Rachel, Edwards, with scarcely a struggle, expired.

The old man fell across the body, the soldier lowered the corse on the couch, and Mahony raising himself on his knees, exclaimed with unsophisticated piety, " May the gates of Heaven open to your soul, sweet Edwards!"

O'Hara was deeply affected with the death of his gallant friend, and obedient to his last wishes (which he found contained in the little paper he had mentioned) made the necessary arrangements for his funeral.

A Serjeant of the deceased's Company arrived, and the commands of his departed Captain were communicated to him. " Deserve the honours of a soldier! Weel does he deserve them," said the veteran. " His fellow he has nae left behind him." O'Hara observing, that as the Regiment was under arms on the Hill, he would procure a detachment from the Garrison of the Citadel to perform the last sad ceremony;——

" Na, na," said the Serjeant, " gin it's necessary, they may fire over him, but nane but his ain shall gie him the last lift. Weel did we stick till him through the day, and his last biddin shall na be left undone. The company's sairly scattered, but there's in the hospital enough to carry him."

The speaker had been a great favourite of his captain, and being beside him when he fell, O'Hara learned from him the distressing, but glorious detail. The light company in many dashing attempts had been driven back with loss. Edwards excited the admiration of the whole; he led his company to the very trenches, and when forced to retire, it was only to return with increased ardour. The colours of the supporting regiment passed frequently to fresh hands, as those who carried them were constantly marked and shot by the riflemen. The last Ensign had fallen, and Edwards seized the fatal standard—a bullet broke the staff and wounded him—he lifted them again, and rushed forward to the redoubt—a second ball struck him in the breast—he staggered to the glacis, threw the colours among the enemy, and sprang headlong over the ditch after them—his company desperately followed. The redoubt was carried with the bayonet, but the bravest of the brave was lost.

A message from Mrs. O'Hara recalled her husband from the chamber of death, and Mrs. Mahony, who conveyed the summons, and her honest Munsterman, met with feelings of undissembled pleasure; she sprang into his extended arms, while fondly pressing her to his bosom, he

exclaimed, " And Fanny, darline, did yourself
ever expect to see me ? We had a busy day,
and, barrin a stragglin shot, I'm as fresh as a
four-year-old ; and may be the master hasn't
got a young son—our turn's next ; but och !
there lies his name-sake—but don't be afeard,
may be you would not fancy to handle a corp,
but a nater one never left a house feet foremost.
M'Dermot lift me over, honey, and the wife
will help us to lay him out. May the gun
burst that kilt him, I pray Jasus !"

The speaker, still pouring out anathemas,
was carried " fornent the captain ;" and his
brother soldier, obedient to his directions, removed a door from its hinges, and on it the
body was extended ; a sash secured it from
moving, and with a quantity of laurel and
other evergreen branches, which had garnished
the apartment, the corse was profusely decorated ; a plate filled with salt was placed on
the breast, and an unequal number of candles
lighted. The Irishmen looked with uncommon
satisfaction at each other, when their task was
completed, and Mahony addressed his coad-
jutor, " M'Dermot, isn't he nately laid out—

och! but his poor mother would be glad to see him. Fanny, love, you luck palish—Mac, my darline, hand her a drap of wine, for crathers in her way is always squamish; but may be, jewel, the mistress would be wanting ye; step over, and after the berril I'll be there too, for the master allowed we would all lie-in together—but see—there's the poor old man (God pity him) whose girl died for love of the Captain, and him gettin the grave dug; well, that's good-natured—it would melt the heart of a stone to hear him afore he died talkin about his sweetheart, but they're now snug in heaven, laughin at us for lamentin them."

The course of Pat's morality was suspended by the measured step of the guard of honour, who now had halted at the door. O'Hara, the officer commanding the party, and Edwards's favourite serjeant, entered, attended by a dozen of the company of the deceased: some of them had been severely wounded—those carried light torches, while the serjeant with the remainder supported the body.

The simple forms of a soldier's funeral are easily arranged, and a low roll of a muffled drum soon announced it to be in motion. The detour to the place of interment was but short, and therefore soon accomplished; and for the first time, and most probably for the last, a military procession passed through the little wicket. The music ceased as it entered, and the corse was silently rested on the grass.

The serjeant, with tears rolling down his hard features, made the wishes of himself and the company known to O'Hara—" The lads wanted their captain's sash and epaulets to share among them for a keepsake."

While these ornaments were removing, a strong gleam of torch-light was thrown on the body, and the face even in death looked beautiful and placid ; the features were perfectly unchanged—the lip was curled as if it still smiled, while here and there its hue of deadly paleness was tinted with a few dark spots of blood. The corse, enveloped in a military cloak, was gently lowered and laid beside her who was yet " green in earth." The mould gradually fell in, and concealed it for ever ; no prayer was read, but many a heartfelt one was uttered. The last melancholy salute was thrice repeated, and the

procession silently retired.   Rachel's father,
with some of his kinsfolk, took an affectionate
leave of O'Hara, who, in profound distress at
the premature death of his gallant friend, hastened from that " end of all men," to seek for
consolation in the smiles of his lovely wife.

CHAPTER V.

Oh! blessed news——
And shall we soon return to the sweet isle we left?

MS. Play.

SOME days elapsed before the extent of the British loss was correctly ascertained. In this battle, so short in duration, with but a small number of troops engaged, the English forces had ninety officers, and upwards of one thousand men, killed and wounded. The Americans suffered comparatively but little, as they estimated their entire casualties at under five hundred men. This disparity in number may be easily accounted for, by the latter having an intrenched position, which, while it sheltered them from the fire of the assailants, afforded a secure rest for the rifle, which on that day was particularly destructive. Four field-officers of distinguished character in the British service fell. Poor old Colonel Abercrombie, with Majors Pitcairn, Williams, and Spendlove. The Americans, in the death of General Warren, lamented a loss, which they justly considered to be irreparable.

Congress in the interim assembled, and resolved that the war should be prosecuted with vigour. The establishment of an army was immediately voted, and a paper currency directed to be issued for its support. The appointment of a general-in-chief was at the same time decreed, and by a numerous vote of the assembly, the celebrated George Washington was summoned from his retirement at Mount Vernon, and invested with this high command. The nomination of a commander-in-chief was followed by the appointment of thirteen subordinate generals. Twelve companies of riflemen were quickly embodied and marched to headquarters, and early in the month of July, Washington himself set out to assume the command of the united forces of the States. On his journey he was every where received with enthusiastic respect, and escorted by volunteer guards of honour, composed of associated gen-

tlemen—congratulated in public addresses by
the principal congress of Massachusets and
New York—the idol of American liberty arrived at the camp of Cambridge.

The British troops still occupied their intrenched position on Bunker's-Hill, defended
on the side next Mystic River by several float-
ing batteries, and on the other by a frigate anchored between Boston and Charleston. The
Americans were encamped on Prospect-hill,
Winter-hill, and Roxbury, each communicating
with the other by small intermediate posts.
General Ward was with the right at Roxbury,
Lee had the left at Prospect-hill, Washington
in person commanded the centre of the revolutionary army. The American general did not
for a moment remain inactive. Boston was
closely blockaded, and all communication with
the country interrupted. The English forces,
confined within the place, were consequently
subjected to many privations, but these they
bore with characteristic fortitude, and it was
determined that the town should hold out to the
last extremity. A period of nearly three months
passed on, the Americans gaining an accession

to their strength daily, and the situation of the army and royalists in Boston becoming still more gloomy. O'Hara had been some time restored to his accustomed health, and Mrs. O'Hara and her infant son were quite well. Mahony had recovered the use of his wounded limb, and his " darline" had produced a chopping boy.

In a few days after the battle of Bunker's-Hill, Captain O'Hara, for his gallant conduct on that occasion, was placed as aid-de-camp on the staff of General Gage. Reinforcements were anxiously expected from England, and never indeed were they more wanted.

In the beginning of September, a frigate arrived with despatches and a Gazette; among the promotions there appeared in the list, " Captain Frederic O'Hara from the forty-seventh regiment, to be major in the twenty-second, vice Miller deceased." This news to Mrs. O'Hara was truly delightful; the twenty-second had just returned a skeleton from foreign service, and were recruiting in Ireland, where they would probably be stationary a considerable time. General Gage was also recalled

F 2

from his command.   With great alacrity the
lady and her attendant commenced the necessary preparations for their departure from a
country to which they had no wish ever to
return.

The vessel which carried out the despatches
was to sail for England immediately, and as
nothing was then more dreaded than a winter
passage across the Atlantic, the Major decided
on embracing this opportunity of returning to
his native country.   With General Gage he
might have come home in a line-of-battle ship,
expected round from Halifax, but he hoped,
by starting without delay, to avoid the stormy
months of October and November.

The baggage of a soldier on service is not
difficult to collect, and although O'Hara's, for
a military establishment, was large, yet the
preparations for his voyage were soon completed.   The morning of their departure arrived—the baggage was already on board—
the wind fair, and the vessel to sail at noon.
O'Hara rose early to write some letters, and
take leave of his brother officers, to whom he
was justly endeared.   On entering the outer

room, he was surprised to find his friend the Scotch Serjeant, who for his gallantry on the 16th, had been just promoted to an ensigncy. The Major and the now commissioned officer met with sincere affection, and the Caledonian having heartily shaken the hand which was offered, mentioned the object of his visit. "They would na let the lads and me place a tomb over the captain, sae I obtained leave to stick a bush o' laurel at his head. The auld body who looks till the place says, he'll have an eye to it, an I guessed you would like till hae a han in the plantin o't." O'Hara thanked him for his attention, and accompanied him to the place where Edwards was interred. The day was just dawning when they reached the gate, and the old man came from his little dwelling beside it, and admitted them. He informed O'Hara, that nothing but the urgent request of Rachel's father could have procured permission for Edwards to be buried there. The erection of any memorial to the dead this simple people considered at best useless and improper, and therefore the wish of the company could not be complied with, but to plant a laurel on his grave was permitted. The old man led to the spot. The commands of the dying soldier had been minutely obeyed, for he and his beloved Rachel were covered by the same turf—there was no division between the graves—one little mound was raised above them both. The serjeant opened the ground, and O'Hara placed the tree in the earth, and they retired unnoticed as they entered. When separating, the Major pressed the old man to accept some money which he presented to him, but he delined it with respect, informing him that his own sect supported him comfortably, and money he neither used nor réquired. The soldiers walked for some time in silence, absorbed in feelings of melancholy originating in a similar cause. The Major commenced the conversation.

" Well, M'Greggor, we have done the last kind office for our friend—Mrs. O'Hara expects us to breakfast—nay, make no excuses; this may be the last day we may be together in this world."

The poor fellow's modesty would hardly allow him to receive the honour which O'Hara insisted on conferring, but the latter was positive. As they returned to the house, the conversation turned on Edwards's successor, the Honourable Gustavus Vining, who had left the Guards for promotion in the forty-seventh. M'Greggor, possessing both the caution of a Scotchman and a soldier, to a stranger would have been profoundly silent, but when the disagreeable subject was broached by the Major, he merely observed—

" To spake o' one's superiors when ye canna spake weel o' them, is better let alane all thegither; certain the change for the men is a sair one—he's na man to fill the shoes o' sic as brave Edwards, but he's a Laird's son or brither, or sic like, and that's enough; but here's Mr. Malowney, who was sae fond o' the poor Captain, to bid ye farewell, and he's the one who cares for neither man or devil (Lord pardon us.")

Breakfast was scarcely ended, when Lieut. Malowney was announced. M'Gregor hastily took leave, observing, as he had the command of the Sally-port Guard, that he would again see his Irish friends. The visiter, as his name

would intimate, was a regularly-bred gentleman of the Connaught school—a plain, healthy-
looking young man, with an active, athletic
figure, good-humoured to a proverb, alternately the entertainer and the butt of the mess-
table; with an acquaintance, nothing—with a
stranger, any thing would ruffle his versatile
temper; a friend might teaze him for a century,
but an enemy dare not trifle with him for a
second—like the wolf-dog of his country, an
infant could ride scathlessly on his back, but
if a man crossed his path, on him he would
turn with ferocity. The pistol he called his
peace-maker; and this same peace-maker was
not allowed to hold a sinecure employment.
Although he was a professed duellist, there
never was a more disinterested one, as he was
always readier to do battle in another's quarrel
than his own. Malowny had a rich vein of
native wit; and when he chose to be severe, his
humour was keen and irresistible. Edwards
and O'Hara were accounted a species of demi-
gods; and amidst his moments of bitterest irri-
tation, a word of kind advice from either would
instantly allay his wrath. The death of the

one, and the departure of the other, affected
him as deeply as his careless, thoughtless disposition would admit of.   He came to pay his
farewell visit, and was entering the room, with
ludicrous melancholy pictured on his countenance, when happening to meet the attendant
going out with the child, he, as a matter of
course, first kissed her, *en passant*, and then
the infant, (who seemed mightily pleased with
the compliment paid to him and his nurse,) and
with a sorrowful face, commenced ;—

   " So you are going away, I hear.   Well,
don't look cross at me for kissing the girl ; and
what am I to do without any body to take care
of me ?   But what an unfortunate devil I have
been since I came to this cursed country ; and
at Bunker's-Hill I was in beautiful luck, wasn't
I ?   Why I saw no more of the fun than if I
had been in Cunemara !   I'm sure it was some
blackguard trying how far his rifle would kill,
that drilled me, for no one was hit but myself
for half an hour after.   All I know is, that I
knew nothing at all till I found myself in my
own bed, and then, at least, I expected the
Company, and what did they do but send that

scare-crow from the Horse-Guards—the devil
bother them for the same; but the regiment
were told to bless God and the Duke, that they
did not make a grenadier of his Lordship. But
there's one comfort—he's in the raven's book,
and his last leave of absence is on the road."

" Pray, are you and he acquainted yet?"

" Oh Lord, yes, intimate as brothers—did'nt
the Colonel bring him in yesterday to the Mess
in one hand, and a croft of toast and water in
the other, for the crature never tastes wine ;
and he talked of St. James's, and field-days in
Hyde-Park, and at eight o'clock his servant
came with a great coat and a muff and tippet,
and some of the lads said that he walked in pat-
tens, to keep his feet from the gravel; but, at
all events, off he set, greatly alarmed for fear
the night air would injure him."

O'Hara laughed at the lively description
which his countryman gave of the successor of
the gallant Edwards.

" But if you had seen him," continued Malowney, " when he showed upon parade—that
exceeded any thing—he was powdered and
pomatumed to the life, and his clothes was what

an Irish tailor calls ' an easy fit,' for they touched him no place ; certainly he was not by when his measure was taken ; and the weight of him—he'll not be hard run to find a charger when he gets the regiment."

The chord of Malowney's humour was struck, and on he went without stopping.

" But yesterday he sent to excuse himself Parade, as he was unwell ; and thought I, its good manners to ask him how he is afterwards, so over I went to his quarters, and found him, large as life, stretched upon a sofa. It was a fine warm day, but he had a blazing wood fire on: up I went, and took him by the hand ; I gave him a bit of a shake, and he roared lustily, ' Easy, easy, my dear Ma—Ma'—' lowney', says I, helping him out with it, for I had nearly shook the breath out of him: by-the-by, I was thinking if he had gone off in the shake, could they have hanged me for murder. Arrah ! what's the matter with your Lordship ? says I. He coughed hard. I'm afraid, says I, your bellows are bad, and if that's the case, when the Spring comes here, you'll go like snow off a ditch.'

" ' Do I look very—very ill, dear Malowney ?'

" ' The devil a worse, says I.'

" ' Oh !' says he, ' it's these pills : I take two in the morning, and they require great care, for there are twelve grains of calomel divided among thirty-six.'

" ' I'll tell you what,' says I, ' you're killing yourself ; let me roll up fifteen or twenty of them in a lump ; swallow that, and it will be the life of you. Why they are only fit for the canary in the corner there.'

" ' Speak lower, my dear fellow,' says he, ' for my head is aching.'

" In came a foreign-looking villain, too rosy in the nose for a water-drinker, with chocolate ; he offered me some, but I told him I preferred spirits and water. His Lordship appeared thunderstruck, and swore it was rank poison. ' It may be so,' says I, ' but it's a slow one, for I have drank it since I was born ; but as may be it's not in the house, there's a bottle on the sideboard that looks like Madeira ; I wouldn't care to taste a drop in a tumbler.' He spoke gibberish to his valet, I'm sure it was not Irish :—the fellow went to the table, and poured a little into the bottom of the glass. Says I, ' I beg your Lordship's pardon, but as I don't speak the languages, will you tell that saffron-faced gentleman to raise his hand a trifle, and help me as as he helps himself.' "

O'Hara laughed, as he exclaimed, " Upon my life, Malowney, you are a most unblushing dog, to treat your commanding Officer, and a Nobleman to boot, with such easy familiarity."

Malowney smiled, and continued ; " Well, in comes Serjeant O'Neill with the orderly-book. What the devil have you there, O'Neill ?" says I.

" ' Nothing strange,' says he, ' only we're expecting some night to be called upon to retake this damned neck, please your honour, which these Yankees have taken a fancy to lately.'

" ' To carry it,' says I, ' won't be very easy.'

" ' Yourself would say that, if you but knew all,' replied the Serjeant. ' It was reconnoitred this morning, and may be, they are not prepared for us ; not content with ditches and shells, they have paraded a row of tobacco hogsheads, filt with rocks and paving stones along

the top*, and when we're coming up, they are
to be rolled down, and as the hill's cruel steep,
they'll come down in a nate canter, and it's no
joke, please your honour (the Serjeant touch-
ing his beaver) to get a puncheon of paving-
stones trundled over a man's carcass.'

" The personage he addressed was mightily
affected. ' Hogsheads, shells, paving-stones,'
he muttered, in rapid succession.

" ' And is there no road but over this cursed
precipice?'

' " Please your Lordship,' said the Serjeant,
' three sides of the hill would bog a snipe, and
the other is as steep as the walls of a windmill.'
His Lordship's cough came on violently, and
declaring that any ascent to him was impracticable, as half a flight of stairs always took away
his breath, I bowed low, and took myself off."

The clock struck eleven; the travellers, equip-
ped for their departure, were shown down by
the landlord with no small regret; for although
he, good man, was too sturdy a Republican not
most mortally to detest any thing bearing a re-

* Gazette, 1775.

semblance to monarchy, yet, in one instance, he made a most marvellous exception, in tolerating the portrait of Majesty, as it appeared on the converse of an English guinea, even to the prejudice of the patriotic but paper currency of his countrymen.

"Come along, Malowney," said the Major, "this last escort was kind of you; I must pass the old 47th, and I would almost rather avoid it." We seldom leave a place where we have resided for some time, without a sensation of regret, even should it not contain any thing to particularly attach us to it; but the party looked on all they passed with total indifference, until through the opening of an alley, the hedge-row of the Quaker's Burying-ground showed for an instant; they paused—and when they proceeded, thought they had then left behind the last object in Boston which could excite even a temporary regret.

Malowney sighed heavily. "I was thinking of Edwards and the Quaker-girl. Wasn't it strange how close he kept the business? Poor fellow! it's a quiet resting-place he's in, but it would be too dull for me. It's the Church-yard of Kilnasallagh that bates the world, and it's there I would like them to plant me. There's not a nicer sod in Connaught for a cock-fight, and the boys have a beautiful gable to play ball against, not forgettin the company coming to drink goats' milk in the morning. The grass is the Sexton's, and his goats flog the country. To be sure, it's not over much frequented of a Sunday, for that's a day of rest; but for the remainder of the week, show me its fellow. Many a day I was flogged for staying from school to court, or play cards on a tombstone."

During Malowney's encomium on the Cone-mara cemetery, the party were approaching the parade-ground of the 47th regiment, and Major O'Hara became visibly affected. At turning the corner, the regiment at once appeared under arms. They were, when they left Ireland, a superior corps, and in their strength and discipline inferior to none in the service. The brave old Colonel was an admirable officer, and had his regiment clean and effective, by discarding as much of the old silly heel-ball and pomatum systems, as the then existing regulations of the British Army would admit. Colonel Coote, his gallant successor, came forward, and most affectionately took leave of Mrs. O'Hara, and then advancing with O'Hara to the front of the regiment, he addressed him ;—

" Major O'Hara—It is a cause of sincere regret, that your promotion could not take place without depriving us of an officer who would reflect honour on any corps to which he was attached. We have known you too long to part with you without heartfelt sorrow ; but we shall take an opportunity of more publicly conveying to you our personal feelings."

A beautiful silver vase was now brought forward by the Adjutant.

" This cup," continued the Colonel, " was presented by General Howe to the 47th Regiment, in testimony of its gallant conduct on the 16th June ; and, by his especial permission, we beg, unanimously, to transfer it to one, who, by his superior bravery, reflected half its glory on the corps which owned him. Forty-seventh present arms !" The regiment, as if to confer an additional honour, performed the command with beautiful regularity ; while, with great emotion, but strong and native eloquence, O'Hara addressed them : his companions in arms listened with profound attention, and when he had ceased speaking, a murmur of applause ran along the ranks.

Mrs. O'Hara's feelings nearly overpowered her. Lieutenant Malowney swore furiously that the Major would die Speaker of the House of Commons ; and Pat Mahony having one hand occupied in holding the vase, was busily employing the other in shaking the hands of all the " Owney jewels," and Dermot honeys, in the Grenadier Company. O'Hara, as he left the ground, felt this, indeed, the proudest moment of his life.

The Colonel escorted the Lady, and the party bent their steps to the barrier, but not without casting " many a longing, lingering look behind." They reached the gate, where Ensign M'Greggor had the guard turned out to receive them with military honours ; and here they took leave of their gallant Colonel. The Ensign, with the permission of the Commanding Officer, accompanied them to the Wharf. The beautiful Bay of Boston was now fully dis-

played to their view, and the ship-of-war in
which they were to embark appeared all ready
for starting, anchored at the distance of half a
mile from the Beach.

O'Hara having fallen back with M'Greggor,
entreated to know if in any manner he could
be serviceable to him: among other plans, he
hinted that of his leaving the Army at some
future time, and settling with him in Ireland.

The Ensign having cleared his throat, said,
with strong emphasis, " I need na sae how
much I feel obligated to you, Major O'Hara, but
I have been too lang in the trade to leave sod-
jering while I'm able to follow it ; and while
my poor Captain lived, nane was happier than
M'Greggor. His death I lament sair. As to
the present man, (beggin his Lordship's pardon,) I suppose he will not mind us much. Mr.
Malowney, and the others, (baith countrymen of
my ain,) are fine pleasant young gentlemen to
serve with."

O'Hara inquired how they agreed in the
Company ?

" Weel, right weel," said the Ensign, " we
are about half and half Irish and Scotch mixed

G 2

thegither, and we agree like brothers. Your lads, Major, are blithe and winsome; better soldiers, and prettier men, never wore a wing—when some odd time they get a bit in liquor, they may be wild and fractious, but they sorrow much afterwards if they hae done ony thing amiss; when they're an service, nane can bare cauld an' hardships merrier; and, by my soul, they are always readier for the fight than the frolic; but here comes the boat."

A barge, pulling eight oars, came rapidly ashore, with a Lieutenant in the stern sheets, to conduct his distinguished passengers on board. The Major and his Lady having affectionately taken leave of their honest escort, embarked with their little suite, and soon the happy party pushed off from the beach, and bade an eternal adieu to the hostile shores of Columbia.

CHAPTER VI.

——————————————————————— The gale aloft
Sung in the shrouds——the sparkling waters hissed
Before, and frothed, and whitened far behind——
Day after day, with one auspicious wind,
Right *from* the setting sun we held our way.
                                      Southey's Madoc.

A MIXTURE of painful and pleasurable feelings
occupied the mind of the Major and his wife,
as they waved a last adieu to their military
friends still lingering on the beach.   This chain
of melancholy musing was broken by the discharge of a gun from the frigate, while, at the
same time, a blue-and-white flag, flying at the
mast-head, disappeared, and the fore-top-sail
was thrown loose,——the well-known signal for
sailing.   The Rosario, to use sea-language,
lay " all-a-tant," and was hove short to a
single anchor, waiting for the boat and passengers.   The barge pulled up rapidly, and,

as it approached the ship, no confusion indicated that any particular business was going forward. The decks and tops were crowded with men, who seemed quite unoccupied ; and such was the silence of all, that a rope's-end striking a timber-head would not have passed unnoticed. At the " weigh—enough" of the lieutenant, the oars were quickly stowed, and the whip, or chair of state, being lowered to receive the lady, she found herself, in a few moments, on board an English frigate, and received in form by the celebrated Captain De Clifford.

The Rosario, of 36 guns, was the finest vessel of that class in the service. She displayed a fine sample of the navy of Great Britain : a beautiful mould,—complete equipment, gallant crew, and dashing commander. De Clifford was promoted to his ship over the heads of many older officers ; but his appointment was as honourable to the Navy-Board as to himself. His short and brilliant career had brought him nobly before the eyes of his country, and the promotion which followed was only due to his deserts. He welcomed his guests with all the ease and openness of a sailor, mingled with the native elegance of a gentleman, which a sincerity in his politeness told was the language more of the heart than the lips.

De Clifford was commonly called in England " the handsome sailor ;" and, as his fair passenger viewed the manly and animated beauty of his face, joined to a tall figure of fine proportions, she thought, excepting her husband, she had never seen so handsome a man.

The boat was taken on board, and the signal made for starting. The crowd of human beings, who but just before were motionless as statues, were, in an instant, actively employed. The anchor was brought to the bows " by the run," the helm put down, and the head-sails set like magic, and, as she canted round, the stops were cast off, the top-sails sheeted home, and the vessel, so lately riding quietly at anchor, was seen, in a few minutes, under a press of sail, standing out of Boston Bay.

Congenial spirits, like the Captain of the frigate, and his military passenger, were soon intimate and attached, and their mutual endeavours to lighten the tedium of the voyage to the lady were so successful, that time flew rapidly, and soundings announced that their passage across the Atlantic was drawing to a close. It was the evening of a blowing day,—the wind was westerly, and the frigate, " hand over hand," was hastening to her destination, when De Clifford spoke with rapturous delight of " England, home, and beauty.". Mrs. O'Hara was employed in finishing a copy of a small pencilled sketch which hung over the cabin chimney-piece, the subject of which had struck her forcibly, as being most singular. It represented an infant, lying on the ground, surrounded by martial trophies and broken arms. In the distance, a party of soldiers were inhuming a female figure, while a warrior, leaning on his sword, gazed with a compassionate look upon the child, who seemed to stretch its little arms to him, and solicit his protection.

" Captain De Clifford, is that drawing the production of your own pencil ? It is a *chef d'œuvre* of its kind."

De Clifford coloured slightly as he replied,
" No ; it is the last memorial of a dear friend.
A messmate of mine gave it to me, and, soon
after, he fell in action by my side. It was my
first, and poor Fielding's *last* battle. Perhaps, for *many* reasons it should be removed ;
but it affords me a melancholy pleasure to see
this memento of my gallant friend, and therefore I retain it."

" May I inquire, if it is merely a creation
of the fancy, or———"

De Clifford appeared confused, and Mrs.
O'Hara blushed, to think her question had
probably been an improper one. After a momentary pause, he added, " To explain the
meaning of that picture, I must communicate
my own history ; and the life of an obscure
sailor cannot be an interesting concern to a
lady."

" Not *an obscure sailor*, certainly," said the
Major.

The Captain bowed, and, with great modesty, mentioned the particulars of his own
story.

His father, the Honourable Henry De Clifford, married imprudently, and being the younger son of a very poor but proud family, was disowned for his folly by his relations; but neither he, nor the cause of his misfortunes, lived to experience the fruits of family displeasure. The regiment went on service, and he fell in the first encounter. The fatal news was incautiously communicated to her; she had just given birth to a boy, and she expired on the second day after. The ill-starred soldier and his wife were interred in one grave.

On the evening of the lady's death, an Irish officer, the Major of the regiment, came to take possession of his effects. Two or three wild-looking women were in the tent, and the poor baby was crying piteously for want of sustenance. " Why do you let the child cry, ye damned brimstones," roared the good-hearted Irishman. " And what have we to say to it ?" " It's hers," said a savage virago, pointing to the corpse in the corner. " Out, ye hags," cried the Hibernian, as he drove them from the tent. " It's a pity," said the Major's man, " to lave the darlin." " Leave it !" said the Master, " who, in the devil's name, would leave it? Lift it gently, Corney, and give Serjeant M'Manus Major O'Shaughnessy's compliments, and I'll give him half my pay, and my blessing, if his woman will give it share of what she has." Corney lifted the orphan, and the Serjeant's wife received it affectionately. The war lasted for several years. O'Shaughnessy wrote frequently to the family of the child, but, as he was but an indifferent scribe, it is probable his epistles never reached their destination.

The desolate infant was often without a shelter. His patron would have nestled him in his heart if he could ; but he very, very often found a shelter for the heads of either unattainable. Peace was concluded, and the Major returned to his own " loved home across the water." But soon his young protégé was fated to be cast again unprotected on the world. In a visit to a friend's house, O'Shaughnessy and a neighbouring gentleman differed in opinion about the colour of a game-cock, and having retired from the table to the field, poor Arthur's friend was mortally wounded by his antagonist. He had only time to send for the boy, and having confessed, now that all was over, that the cock was a *custard dun,* (but he would scorn to have acknowledged it, till after a shot,) he informed those who surrounded him of Arthur's history, and, having forgiven his sorrowful opponent, and made him promise to carry the infant to his family, expired, invoking blessings on the youthful mourner.

His promise to the dying man was faithfully performed by the repentant homicide : he conveyed the child, now four years old, to England, and, having learned that the noble family he sought were at their magnificent château on the Sussex coast, with a splendid party visiting them, O'Connor determined to introduce his charge with due publicity. The Earl, he was told, was high and haughty; but, had be been the devil himself, the Milesian would not have shrunk from his engagement. Arriving at the next village, he learned that the Prince of ——— was there. O'Connor dressed himself and the boy in their best apparel, and, taking him in one hand, and a stout cudgel in the other, proceeded to execute the commands of his deceased opponent. He reached the house just as dinner had ended, and, on asking for the Earl, was sturdily told by the porter, that he was engaged with his betters. Directed by the noise, the janitor, with amazement, perceived the intruder leisurely crossing the hall, and, most unceremoniously, entering the banquetting-room; but his astonishment was far surpassed by the effect of the appearance of this curious phenomenon on those within, as he announced himself to the haughty group around the table,—" Here I am, Roderic O'Connor, of Slishmeen, your Royal Highness's most obedient servant till death——Here, my Lord Earl, is your well-looking grandson. Down on your knees, jewel, and ask the old boy's blessin : and here are the proofs, as he laid down the crab-tree to pull a roll of smoke-dried papers from his side-pocket. Hands off, you staring blackguards, till I tell all about it. No noise ; for here I stand in the presence of my Prince, and Roderic O'Connor demands justice for the child of Captain Henry De Clifford."

The party was strangely surprised, and the servants utterly confounded. In a few words O'Connor told his simple story. The Earl took the child in his arms, and the Prince kissed his cheek. The lord of Slishneen was invited to sit down, and with that easy assurance attributed to the character of Ireland, he soon felt himself quite at home; and, after a sojourn of a few days, during which he exhibited to the delighted party all the unbridled vivacity of an unschooled Milesian, he took his leave of the child, and, with a lightened heart, returned to his castle of Slishmeen.

But the orphan's fate was still to be thrown friendlessly on strangers. In three years, the Earl died of apoplexy, without making any provision for young Arthur; and when it was quite uncertain, whether any of his cold-hearted uncles would deign to think of the desolate child, an old friend of his father's, Commodore Sir Joshua Hardyman arrived, and, by accident, became acquainted with the circumstances of the family. He tendered his interest and protection, and it was readily accepted. Sir Joshua, though illiterate himself, decided on giving a suitable education to his protégé. He, accordingly, sent him to school, where, after remaining five years, he had him rated midshipman. Arthur soon after accompanied the Commodore to the West Indies on board the Tremendous, of eighty-four guns, then carrying his flag as commander of that station.

It is unnecessary to follow the young De Clifford through all the brilliant achievements which distinguished his splendid career. Sir Joshua remarked and rewarded them by successive promotions; and now, at the commencement of a profitable war, he started for fame and fortune, in the command of the finest frigate destined for the American coast.

There was a strange coincidence between De Clifford and his father. He was also married, and report added—imprudently. The lady was a portionless woman of family, and extravagant to a blamable degree. She lived in London, and the pay and prizes of her gal-

lant husband, (some of which were considerable,) were supposed quite insufficient to defray
the prodigality of his wife. She never accompanied him to sea; and, it was whispered, that
even the very limited periods which the duties
of the service allowed him to indulge in on
shore, were imbittered by her cold and un-
amiable disposition.

Although many an hour was spent by him
in talking of his "beloved wife," yet it was
evident that at times he was far from happy.
These feelings were as studiously concealed as
they could be, and the most that he ever ven-
tured to hint on this agonizing subject, was,—
"a pity poor Lady Sarah had been so expen-
sively brought up: she was so generous, so
unsuspicious, so charitable, that her small
pittance was scarcely adequate to her wants;
and, on his return from sea, he usually found
her in little difficulties." From these unhappy
recollections, he would turn to his child, then
two years old, and the delight her remembrance recalled assisted in banishing from his
mind the misconduct of her parent. "Poor
fellow!" sighed O'Hara, as the Captain was

suddenly called upon deck, " I fear it is a cold and gloomy home you hasten to !"

The wind blew fair and steadily till the Rosario dropped her anchor in Plymouth harbour, nineteen days from the time she last weighed it. Here the brave friends parted for ever. De Clifford, with all the rapidity of four horses, started for London with the despatches, and O'Hara directed his course, by easy stages, to Holyhead, to embark in the packet for Dublin.

To be once more on English ground in safety, accompanied by him who had induced her to leave it, was a subject of unqualified delight for the fair voyager. The Major was now recalled from foreign service, and she looked forward to the termination of this destructive war with the Colonies, or her own gentle influence, ultimately succeeding in withdrawing him from a military life. The blessed security of a land internally at peace formed a striking contrast to the unfriendly aspect of the shores they had quitted. Cooped within the narrow compass of a blockaded town, or confined on shipboard, the liberty

of an open country was glorious as exhilarating. The peasantry were comfortable and
contented,—the farm-yards frequent and profusely filled with corn,—and, as she viewed
the peace and plenty which surrounded her,
she rapturously exclaimed,—" Oh ! who, for
the bubble reputation, would leave the blessings of a British hearth ?" Her husband
sighed, as he folded up the newspaper he had
been perusing. There the state of Ireland was
rather mysteriously slurred over. It was a
ministerial print, and, from the slovenly manner certain political circumstances were passed
by, O'Hara augured that the tranquillity of
his native land was not unbroken ; but, feeling
the spell must of necessity be soon dissolved,
he forbore to cloud the sunny moment of
return, by breathing the probability of a
doubtful future. On landing in Dublin, he
found his fears confirmed : he had only left
one land of civil commotion for another. Ireland was wretchedly agitated. A heavy and
portentous storm had been long collecting,
and none could say when or where it would
burst.

We shall pass over for some years the common-place detail of the life of O'Hara, and the infancy of his son, to give a rapid sketch of the history and politics of the country. This was, indeed, a stormy period, and the eventful year of 1799 will be long remembered.

England found herself engaged in a triple conflict,—America, France, and Spain, were united against her. The combined fleets of the two latter powers, unawed by the Channel fleet, inferior to them in strength and number, threatened the coasts of Great Britain with invasion, while the remote and unguarded parts of Ireland and Scotland remained in momentary apprehension of descents from numerous privateers, which, having almost annihilated a declining commerce, followed and destroyed the shipping in the harbours, or landed openly on the coast to plunder the houses of the wealthy. The existence of the Government was a subject of critical apprehension, and could be continued only by a mighty resistance ; and in order to prevent the country from becoming the theatre of a doubt-

ful conflict, it was deemed imperative by the
Ministry of the day to endeavour to keep the
battle at a distance. The exertions necessary
to effect this indispensable measure drained the
kingdom of its soldiery, and thus no alterna-
tive was left to the Parliament but to remove
the military force so requisite at the time for
its defence, and abandon the country to its
fate. The maritime towns, fearful of plunder
and destruction, called on the Government to
assist them, but were answered that no troops
could be spared, and their protection must be
confided to themselves. In consequence of
this communication, a numerous and respectable body of citizens were embodied, and,
aware that the public finances were in a state
of bankruptcy, they at individual expense
clothed and armed themselves ; while the Executive, delighted at the spirit of determined
resistance then happily pervading the Irish
people, encouraged it by their approval, and,
to give it effect, dispensed an immense quantity of arms and military stores throughout
the kingdom.

Here was the origin of the volunteers of

Ireland ; and be it remembered, to their immortal honour, that although organized and
disciplined by themselves, they not only paid
profound deference to the laws, but frequently
and zealously interfered in having them impar-
tially and faithfully executed.

The advantages and defects of this once
celebrated institution have been frequently
canvassed, and very differently decided on.
Their day has long passed by, but they will
not soon be forgotten. It will be sufficient to
observe generally, that as a military association they deterred their Gallic neighbours
from an invasion ; while the internal peace and
tranquillity of the country was in an eminent
degree preserved by their vigorous exertions,
and the willing co-operation given by this
body to the unbiassed administration of justice.

The utility of the volunteers has been universally acknowledged ; few have doubted the
purity, none the patriotism of the system ; but
as their numbers were imposing, and their
influence unbounded, the Government soon
had cause to view them with apprehension and

distrust. The members of this popular institution speculated loosely in the politics of the
times, and, as their enemies alleged, deviated
from their original object by forming provincial meetings for the avowed purpose of discussing questions of parliamentary reform ; and
whilst protesting against the abuses of the
Constitution, they pressed, and probably too
strongly, upon Ministers the necessity of restoring it to its pristine purity. In further-
ance of these principles, the Dungannon Convention assembled on the 15th February, 1782.
Their resolutions were most determined in de-
manding a speedy reform, and a more general
diffusion of the rights of civil liberty. No
wonder the Government felt that there was
more of dictation than prayer in the petition,
for their opinions were delivered with the boldness of delegates, the representatives of one
hundred thousand men in arms.

The example of the volunteers of the North
was followed by the meeting of the delegates
of Leinster, in the month of the ensuing October ; and, as a finale, the grand National
Convention, comprising delegates from every

corps in Ireland, assembled at the Royal Exchange in the metropolis, on the 10th November, 1783.

Previous to this period, the volunteers in many places had invited the Roman Catholics to associate and take up arms. A corps of great strength, called the Irish Brigade, was accordingly embodied, and it was resolved, at a meeting of delegates, that the training of every class of Irishmen to the use of arms was a measure of vital importance to the country. In pursuance of this resolution, a regular drill was established, and, in the summer, an encampment formed at Roebuck, in the county of Dublin, in which the Irish Brigade, and the Volunteers of the City, practised camp and military duties, and all the manœuvres connected with active service.

In the north of Ireland, the Presbyterians had been for many years firmly united to the Americans, and the principles of the new Republic were universally admired by a considerable proportion of the inhabitants of Ulster. The subsequent events strongly proved that the period elapsing between the declara-

tion of the independence of the United States
and the era of the French Revolution had
confirmed these democratic feelings.

It will be necessary here to remark, that for
several years prior to 1792, this part of Ireland was constantly disturbed by the religious animosities of the Dissenters and Roman
Catholics.   After the volunteering system had
gradually expired, the former, becoming jealous of the latter party's retaining a vast
quantity of arms in their possession, which
they had instructed them to use, frequently
assembled during the night for the purpose of
disarming their quondam associates ; the Presbyterians assuming the title of "Peep-o'-day-
boys," the others adopted the name of "Defenders."   The passions of the contending
parties being artfully inflamed by the leaders,
no opportunity of exercising mutual animosity
was suffered to escape.   Many severe skir-
mishes ensued ; at last, after several ineffec-
tual attempts had been made towards a reconciliation, the hostile parties came to a general
engagement, at a place called "the Diamond,"
on the 21st September, 1795, which termi-

nated in the entire defeat of the Defenders, who were driven from a strong position, after numbers of their friends had been killed or wounded.

To commemorate this victory, the first *Orange Lodge*, composed exclusively of Protestants, was instituted.

We now return to O'Hara: the regiment in which he had gotten his promotion, after having been for some time at Belfast, was ordered to Dublin, and there remained for two years, doing garrison duty. The Major had therefore many opportunities of visiting his estate in the north. Soon after they had been removed to the metropolis, Mrs. O'Hara was delivered of a second son, who survived its birth but a few days. The lady's confinement had been very unfavourable, and in consequence her health became so much impaired, that an immediate change to her native air was prescribed, as necessary for her recovery. The Major, tired of an inactive military life, and aware that the health and happiness of his wife required it, determined, after mature deliberation, to leave the army and retire on

the half-pay list.   Many things tended to induce him to adopt this measure : his estate
was most improvable, situated in a wild and
romantic country, and yet contiguous to several respectable market-towns.   Accordingly,
he   memorialized   the   Commander-in-Chief,
who, in consideration of his brilliant, though
short services, acceded to his retirement, and
gazetted him out on full pay.

The Ex-Major, therefore, in the latter end
of 1778, bade adieu to the honourable trade
of arms, and with his lady and his young son,
took possession of the mansion of his forefathers.

CHAPTER VII.

Yet he's gentle; never school'd, and yet learned; full of
noble device; of all sorts enchantingly beloved.

As You Like It.

CASTLE CARRA was wild and lonely in its situation ; it stood on a bold eminence, over-
looking the narrow union of two extensive
lakes, on one side, while on the other it was
surrounded by a cordon of rocky hills, rising
above each other in alternate ridges, till the
black and broken summits of the Mourne
mountains topped the entire, and threw a
duskier shade upon the heaths beneath them.
The edifice was in perfect preservation ; the
ornamental parts of the building, its turrets,
narrow arched doors, and gothic casements,
executed with that beautiful regularity which
characterizes the designs of former artists,
displayed the same appearance they had done

two hundred years before. The roof was
flagged with grey-stones ; the doors were
oaken, and studded with iron bolts ; the windows filled with glass of dark and gloomy
colours ; the whole looking strength without
comfort, pride without magnificence. No
alteration in its appearance was observable, as
any repairs which time had rendered necessary
were effected without taking aught from its
antiquity. The offices detached from the main
building were partly sunk in a ravine, and
partly shaded by the tall trees that embo-
somed them. Clumps of oak-trees and scrub
(as the lower Irish term coppice-wood) were
interspersed over the distant heaths. The
castle towered above the whole, and from the
high bank on which it stood forced itself upon
the view with an imposing air of gloomy iso-
lated grandeur. A broad ditch, once filled with
water, encompassed the ancient fortress ; but
the later owners had given the stream another
direction, and, levelling the mounds, clothed
their sloping sides with verdure, while the river
which had supplied the fosse, diverted from
its original channel, fell a little to the right

into the lake, wandering in its course through
shrubberies and extensive gardens. The lakes
extended fourteen or fifteen miles, and were
irregular in their breadth, varying from one to
seven. The extremities of neither were visible, as the prospect terminated by the head-
lands shutting in on either side. The castle,
being placed on the narrow strait, where the
waters of both united, had been erected to
command the ancient bridge, a pass at that
time undoubtedly of great importance.

In the retirement of Castle Carra, Henry
O'Hara was educated. The boy, from his
infancy, seemed destined to support some arduous character in the drama of human life :
his constitution, his form, and his youth, were
all extraordinary for his years. The contiguous heaths afforded him health and exercise ; sickness or restraint had never prevented
him from braving each opposite of heat and
cold ; and, attended by his tutor, more as a
companion than a guide, he wandered wherever
fancy prompted.

The period of infancy is soon passed over ;
years roll on rapidly, and that portion of ex-

istence comprised between childhood and ado-
lescence is but remembered as a dream.   The
mother of young O'Hara had been removed
before her son could well estimate her loss,
and his surviving parent devoted himself
wholly to the education of the orphan ; but of
necessity, it was, in many material points, wild
and imperfect.   The seclusion of his father,
and the solitude of the mansion, had given a
romantic turn to the habits and opinions of
the son, and when he had completed his fifteenth year, he knew men as he was taught
mathematics,—solely by the agency of others.

The ill health of Mrs. O'Hara had made
Dr. Molloy a constant visiter at the castle :
from the child's infancy the physician had
been attached to him, and so sincerely, that
when he lost his mother, the Doctor retired
from practice, and took up his residence at
Castle Carra, where he had been an inmate
for many years.   Dr. Molloy had crept into
life from great obscurity, and his youth had
passed away before he obtained the requisite
qualifications for practising physic.   To a
figure of singular oddity, he united uncouth

manners ; the exterior was harsh and repulsive,
but the feeling heart it contained was inesti-
mable. Kindness and innocence were buried
beneath the rough and unpolished habits of
his youth ; and when his breast throbbed as he
listened to a tale of misery, his features at the
moment would have pictured gloomy misan-
thropy, although a dole, too liberal for his
limited fortune to warrant, was dealt with an
unsparing hand. Nature had refused her
favours to his person, but she had been otherwise munificent. A comprehensive mind, and
prodigious memory, gifted this self-taught
scholar ; and while his abstracted manners would
have admitted a charge of downright stupi-
dity, perhaps at the moment this singular
being was lost in contemplations from which
minds of no ordinary capacity would have
shrunk with dismay. As a professional man,
his character stood justly high ; and, consequently, the liberal and extensive practice he
had possessed enabled him to exert his benevo-
lent dispositions, and acquire a moderate independence. He was fond of society, although
his unconquerable absence of mind often in-

commoded him in conversation, and his wandering thoughts could never be sufficiently at
home to allow him to engage at the card-table.
In the drama he delighted, and as he listened
to the strollers who occasionally visited the
adjoining market-town, to him the delusion of
the scene disappeared, and all was truth and
reality. On one occasion he interrupted the
business of the stage by throwing a handful of
silver to " Lieutenant Workington," and even
once arrested the fate of the gentle Désde-
mona, by striding over the benches, and shout-
ing, " Othello, you're a fool!" and tendered
his oath to the exculpation of the suspected
beauty. His was a character constructed of
opposites ; one moment grappling with a folio,
and the next bewildered in the intricacies of
a romance. He wrote much, but his lucubra-
tions were usually committed to fate and shreds
of paper. He had once, indeed, gone so far as
to send a clever work into the world, notwithstanding arrangement was not to be included
among the number of its excellencies. Every
one in the neighbourhood subscribed to what,
with one or two exceptions, no one in the

neighbourhood could understand. But none
of these patrons of genius ever thought of
sending any equivalent,—to wit, the cash:
this latter, he ("good easy man,") overlooked
—the patrons and publisher shared the profit,
and the disciple of Æsculapius was permitted
to pay the incidental expenses. Such was
young Henry's tutor; and under him he was
likely enough to become a ponderous scholar;
but parental solicitude, perceiving that something was necessary to correct the same failing
so discernible in the preceptor, determined
O'Hara to sacrifice his love of retirement to
the interests of his child, and introduce him to
the world. To the University he turned his
thoughts, and concluded by placing his name
on the books, and attending to the progress of
his studies there. A house was accordingly
provided in Clare-street, and with reluctance
he prepared to bid adieu to the seat of his
ancestors, and enter once more on a world, to
which he had lately supposed he had bidden
an eternal farewell.

Since the decease of Mrs. O'Hara, a clumsy
offer had been made by her brother towards a

reconciliation.   O'Hara generously met these
advances, and extended the " olive-branch" to
his undeserving relative ; and, anxious to
show how sincerely he intended, he nominated
young Moore (then admitted to the practice of
the law) his agent, and established him with a
liberal salary in his new office.   This act of
generous and kind confidence was requited as
it did not merit; and an ill-fated reliance
reposed in his false and wily kinsman, proved
eventually ruinous to the fortunes of his son.

The morning of the departure of the
widower was one of real sorrow ; the carriage
drew up to the hall-door ; it was the same
Mrs. O'Hara had used during her life, and
this was the first time it was employed by her
husband, to convey him from a spot hallowed
by her remembrance.   The Major was deeply
affected ; tears coursed each other down his
manly cheek, and while Molloy blessed his
pupil, and cursed and cried alternately, the
carriage started.   The traveller threw himself
back in an agony of distress, while Henry, in
a mingled mood of joy and sorrow, watched
the old gates closing—his solitude was de-

serted, and now " the world was all before
him."

The period of young Henry's entrance into
Dublin was fated to behold that city in the
zenith of its greatness ; glittering amid an
halo of surrounding splendour, like the tropi-
cal sun, glorious to the last, its brilliancy was
scarcely shaded for a moment, when it sunk in
the waters for ever. The opulence and beauty
of the Irish capital ranked it inferior to few
cities in the world. Then, a native Parliament was assembled, and scarcely was there a
man of rank and affluence in the kingdom who
had not a winter residence in the metropolis
Public and private amusements were conse
quently splendid ; routes were every night to
be heard of ; the carriages of the nobility and
gentry thronged the squares ; flambeaux glittered in the streets, and Venice and its carni-
val was often emulated by the festive gaiety of
the city of the " Emerald Isle." What a
mournful contrast was it fated to exhibit !
Ten short years saw it splendid and wealthy—
deserted and undone ! The contemplation is

I 2

sickening,——like that melancholy air of Swit-
zerland which maddens, by its reminiscence of
lost liberty, those who were once free. Dublin
as it was, and as it is.———But we shall not
carry on these unhappy recollections.

The court of 1792, nearly equalled St. James's
in splendour and display. The first and haugh-
tiest in the empire trode its carpets, and few,
very few, of that nameless multitude, whom
lack of better afterwards introduced, were
ever seen within its halls. The table was
crowded with bidden guests; but, " woe worth
the day," now the highways and streets are
forced to contribute their quota, and eke out
a lamentable deficiency with paupers or ple-
beians. The Irish court, preserving a semblance of royalty, *then* deferred to birth and
talent. Now and then, when a whimsical
vicegerent presided, a mercer, or music-master
suffered knighthood in a drunken frolic ; but,
not presuming on the solemn mockery, and
feeling the bitter irony of their elevation, Sir
John's voice was never loud, but in the
choir; while the only alteration in Sir James

was, a more than common adroitness in slipping his scissars through the lutestring,—like the unschooled tuition of Scrub, when he wished to rival his " brother Martin" at the knife-board, the good knight's envy and emulation never ranged beyond the confines of Skinner-row ; but *tempora mutantur*,—that is, the tables are turned,—and nothing so plenty in the metropolis, as knights and empty houses.

To a person returning after an absence of some years, the wonderful change in the occupations of the streets would forcibly strike him,—" To what uses may we not return !" At that time, the beautiful row of houses in Sackville-street was undisfigured by shop or show-board ; neither huge Elephant, nor tawdry Chinese merchant, had existence. The brass plates upon the doors informed the reader, that a Lord, or Lady, or M. P., was the occupant. But now, alas ! names and trades glitter from the attic to the area ; and the coronetted carriage has given place to the grocer's cart. Can Dublin yet sink lower ? Is degradation not consummated ?

Impossible ! unless some Sultan Mahmoud, of devastating propensities, would altogether qualify it to dower some portionless screech-owls.

Let no reader here imagine, that I make these observations, as in any way contemning trade and its followers. Far be it from me. I myself am a member of one of the humblest classes of society, and would not, therefore, despise any individual of the community. I have passed through life, (praise be to God,) without even an attempt having been made to subject me to the pains and penalties of knighthood. I have, furthermore, cause to be thankful, for (although I do not wish to vaunt me of my good fortune,) I never was appellated Esquire but once, and that by the mistake of a Methodist preacher, persuaded by a wag, to apply to me on a begging occasion, as a well-known contributor to Gospel ministers and conventicles. For this good luck, I suppose myself indebted to my youthful days being gone by, before the Esquire epidemic had broken out with its present violence. Last Saturday, as I strolled along the banks of the royal canal, I picked up a letter with a barbarous superscription, purporting to direct the enclosure, "To Fill Ruggins, Esquare, No. 2½, Cross Poddle." Ah! I understand it. Some young spendthrift on his keeping. I will deliver it myself. I made out Phil Ruggins, Esq., forthwith, at his residence, 2½, Cross Poddle; and, by Heaven! he was a journeyman bobbin-weaver. But what has Phil Ruggins to say to this story?

I was, I remember, speaking of Dublin Castle; and, like the etiquette of the said castle, one story shall introduce another, and, therefore, one anecdote more of myself, (I am a little egotistical to-day). Many a time, with a lady on either arm, Mrs. Timothy Flin, of the Weaver's-square, and Mrs. Peter Dunlavy, of Mark's-alley, have I left the liberty in the evening, to view the grandees, as they went in state to the drawing-room. Corkhill was our favourite station, and there, among apprentices, mantua-makers, and ladies' waiting-women, known to the mob by the familiar title of "kitchen stuff," have we gazed with admiration, on the showy equipages, at one moment at a dead stand, and at the next, with rapid motion jerking themselves into the vacancy occasioned by the last set-down. Nor were we permitted to look on with impunity. Pickpockets were on the alert, while, now and again, a grenadier, with a charged bayonet, and " Stand back, blast yees," made an awful irruption into our terror-struck squares. Last week I read among the list of presentations, the names of Mrs. Henry Rourke, and Mrs. T. P. Reilly. Often have they gazed from these arms, till they ached, on passing peers and peeresses. The former was Julia Dunlary: the latter, Matilda Henrietta Flin.

Will another story be tolerated? I hate apologies, so I shall give it without any. I wanted stockings, (by, the by, my washer-woman accuses me of great severity on the heel,) and had recourse to an eminent hosier's to refit. It was dusk, and all the neighbouring shops were closing. I hate haggling with a shop-keeper: the bargain was soon concluded,—the stockings in paper,—and my one-pound-note undergoing a severe scrutiny on the counter. " Mat!" cried a shrill voice from the farther end of the shop. Matthew started. " Mat, my dear!" Matthew became more composed. " Send James to the row for our carriage,—Sir Thomas's coach is at the door, and his shutters on this half hour,—don't mind the pickle people,—ever since his wife was *persented*, she makes it a rule to be an hour later than the world. Ah, Mat! if you took the right side in the hall, I would have been *interduced* long ago." The truth is, Mat is a common council-man, but having a bad drop in him, (his grandmother was a papist,) he did not roar, with the remainder, against the *Roman bill*,—and I can assure the hosier's lady, that she will never, in the drawing-room of Dublin Castle, elbow Mrs. Nelligan, of the pickle warehouse, unless the aforesaid Mat entertains more orthodox sentiments of the damnable doctrines of Pope and Popery !

CHAPTER VIII.

That Lord Fitzwilliam's viceroyalty would have banished
all discontent I cannot suppose; but, that if the Catholic
claims had been settled, or some parliamentary reform taken
place, rebellion would not have reared its head, I am willing
to believe.

Hardy's Life of Charlemont.

RETIRED from the busier scenes of former life,
O'Hara watched in its progress the arduous
struggle for freedom beyond the Atlantic, until
the consummation of the hopes and independence of America was achieved by those whom
oppression had determined to be free. The
insane policy of ministers was persevered in till
all their misconduct could effect was completed;
they severed the colonies from the parent—
raised a mighty power into political existence,
which, had common moderation been granted to
their supplication, would have been contented
to have remained auxiliary and dependent,—and

taught a lesson of liberty to the world, which often afterwards made monarchy tremble on the throne.

In this contest for freedom, glorious in its issue, O'Hara had to lament the fall of many of his former companions in arms; and in the last effort made by the royal army to relieve itself from the miserable dilemma into which the ability of the American leaders had drawn it, before safety was secured by an unavoidable surrender, Malowney and M'Greggor fell. The Highlander, by exemplary conduct, had attained the rank of captain; and Malowney's luck, as he termed it, having carried him in safety through many a bloody conflict, at length deserted him, when in the command of the forty-seventh regiment, to which he had pushed his way by dint of sheer fighting, without owing a single compliment to either duke or minister. He made his exit from the stage of life in the most summary manner, in an attempt to force the American lines at Saratoga. A bullet in the brain to many would not have been particularly desirable, but honest Dennis was no man for round-about measures, and probably felt this mode of bidding "his long good night" just as agreeable as in having his last sands eked out under the cautious directions of a regular physician.   He fell not in victory, but the attempt was well planned and boldly exe-cuted ; and, like Montgomery dying before the barriers of Quebec, even in death and defeat he left a gallant name behind him.

The death of Mrs. O'Hara in 1786, seemed to be the opening of her husband's misfortunes, and from that time his destinies became gradu-ally overcast.   The precarious health of his la-mented consort had for years before her death precluded any close intimacy from subsisting between Castle Carra and the gayer world. The remote situation of the mansion rendered distant visiting impracticable to an invalid ; but the high crime of inhospitality (a grievous sin amongst the Irish) did not attach its stigma to its hall.   The castle was not without visiters, and as O'Hara took a leading part in the poli-tics of these times, many names, afterwards fatally distinguished in the field and on the scaffold, were found among his intimates.   Lord Edward Fitzstephen, Wolfe, Russell, O'Moore,

O'HARA. 125

and others of the democratic leaders, composed
a group of attached associates.   There the occurrences of these stormy times were discussed
or arranged—there the necessity of reform was
enforced—there election opposition to county
aristocracy was embodied; in fine, the retirement
of O'Hara was the focus whence the Whigs and
Reformers incessantly poured forth their remon-
strances, and fulminated resolutions and protests.
. . Among the many friends of O'Hara, there
was one to whom he was particularly attached.   At the termination of the American
war, Fitzstephen returned to Ireland; he was
then a very young man, and a captain in the
fifteenth regiment.   During the contest with
the States, he served with distinguished reputation, and gave early promise of possessing
those military talents which afterwards gained
him a melancholy celebrity.   With the soldiery
he was frank, condescending, and humane;
while in the hour of danger, each felt safety
and assurance in the unmoved bearing of their
chivalrous leader.   He bore fatigue and the se-
verities of climate with unalterable composure;
and obstacles, which had hitherto bounded the

attempts of all, gave way to his enterprise and determination.   He seemed to be the very chief of the Poet—

Who shall lead a host
From India's fires to Zembla's frost.

O'Hara and Fitzstephen became acquainted on service—both were soldiers, and both enthusiasts—their opinions on the subject of civil and religious liberty alike, and their advocacy of its justice bold, warm, and unguarded.   Fitzstephen, at the time we mention him, was probably thirty years old ; his figure, though small, was perfectly well formed ; his hair and complexion of the deepest brown, his eyes dark and penetrating, his carriage free and active, his step soldierly ; such was the exterior—but let those who remember him complete the portrait—the mind gifted and intelligent ; the manner exquisitely polished, but warm, wild, and winning ; his honour unblemished as his beauty—but surely Lord Edward, in Ireland, is not forgotten !

To recall to the memory of his country his virtues and misfortunes (and they were many) would be unnecessary ; his crimes have received

the fiat of another tribunal—we trust and believe they were but few—peace to his ashes!

The year 1795 opened with prospects of
conciliation, which alas! were transitory and
delusive. An appointment to the chief government of Ireland had taken place, from which
much advantage was expected to arise. Lord
Fitzwilliam succeeded Lord Westmoreland, and
one *, who to the last was faithful to the country which gloried in him, gave the discontented
strong assurance that the reign of bigotry was
drawing to a close. The Viceroy landed in
Dublin on the 4th of January, and no time
was lost by the Roman Catholics in preparing
a petition, praying for a removal of the disabi-
lities under which they suffered. In this appeal
to the House the northern Presbyterians heartily
concurred; a majority of the Protestants supporting the catholic claims from principle, while
many, who had hitherto studiously avoided
interference in political affairs, but now,
conscious that the ferment of public opinion
required some sedative to allay its violence,
stepped forward to join their voice to the ge-

* Henry Grattan.

neral call made on the government for justice.
This was the last effort of Ireland, and it was
blasted.   Lord Fitzwilliam was suddenly called
from his government, leaving an abused people
without one ray of hope to gild the darkness of
their despondency.   What must have been the
deep sorrow of the Reformers and Roman Catholics in seeing him removed from the lieute-
nancy, may be conjectured from the character
given of him by the most bigoted and credu-
lous chronicler of the times*:—" From the re-
spectability and amiableness of his character,
no person could doubt the rectitude of his in-
tentions; or that he had any other object at
heart than the interest of the empire—but it is
believed that his lordship was unacquainted
with the real state of the kingdom."

The hopes of the Roman Catholics had been
raised to the pinnacle of expectation, and on the
destruction of their high prospects, they gave
way to anger and despair.   A deputation from
the catholic board hastened to St. James's; but
their remonstrance was coldly received by the
king, and the Duke of Portland referred the

* Musgrave, page 161.

prayer of their petition to " those dreadful
guardians" who had succeeded Earl Fitzwilliam—" that combination" (to use the
words of the lamented Grattan) " which galled
the country with its tyranny—insulted her by
its manners—exhausted her by its rapacity, and
slandered her by its malice." The new government instantly proceeded to visit the malecontents with cruel and unjustifiable severity :
under the plea of security, the metropolis was
rendered intolerable to all but the minions of
the administration ; while, with the pretence of
restoring social order, Lord Carhampton re-
paired to the midland and western counties,
and alleging that the laws were inoperative in
them, " resolved to restore their energy by"
what Sir Richard calls " a salutary system of
severity." He assembled the principal Orange-
men of each county, and having in concert with
them, examined the charges against the leaders
of this banditti, who were in prison, but defied
justice, (*anglicè*, persons against whom no
shadow of evidence could be produced to warrant their conviction,) he, with the concur-
rence of these gentlemen, sent the most nefari-

ous of them on board a tender stationed at
Sligo. By this bold measure, founded on obvious principles of political necessity, he completely restored peace in the disturbed districts.
This unparalleled outrage on Irish liberty
elicited universal deprecation; and, arbitrary
as the government was, it soon found itself
unequal to shelter the engine of its tyranny
against the numerous civil actions which were
in progress against him, till, by the unprece-
dented measure of resorting to a bill of indemnity, the unhappy sufferers had their wrongs
and hopes of redress equally silenced for ever.
This infamous bill passed, after a furious opposition, early in 1796. Fitzstephen in his place
in the Commons, and O'Hara at a county meeting, delivered their opinions of these unconsti-
tutional proceedings with a freedom of deprecation which gave mortal offence to the Irish
court. At this period, January, 1796, we
resume our private memoir.

It is probable that O'Hara's resolution of
passing some time in the Irish capital was confirmed by the advice of Lord Edward. The
friends who had associated at Castle Carra

were once more assembled in Clare-street. The
character of the times was now taking an imposing aspect—discontent was too loud and too
determined not to bring on a speedy crisis. The
organization of United Irishmen, from the moment of its birth, had become truly formidable,
and the government at last saw their danger.
Had they gone too far to conciliate? Could
not the storm, which had been so long gather-
ing, and whose explosion was no longer to be
reckoned an uncertainty, be mitigated by gentle
measures, and its violence dispersed by those
whose mal-administration had first raised it?
This question was not deemed worthy of consideration, or if it was, an opposite conclusion
was the result.

With the personages more than the politics
of these days our business lies, and in a short
summary we shall comprise the history of these
unhappy times. From the period of 1792, the
lower classes of the Reformers were in commotion, and the higher dissatisfied. French
politics gained ground apace; mobs of great
numerical force frequently assembled, and were
only dispersed by military interference and

K 2

mutual loss of lives. The discontent of the
lower Irish was further augmented by the passing of the Militia Bill : the disaffection of the
higher confirmed by espionage, arrests, and
ex officio prosecutions. A clergyman of the
establishment, to avoid the ignominy of a public
execution, perished by poison at the bar; while
many of the leading malecontents saved their
lives by a voluntary expatriation. Military
license and tyranny became intolerable—suspected persons were seized, and sent on board
the royal navy, without even the mockery of
investigation—houses were searched for arms,
and should the inmates be absent, they were denounced as rebels, and their property consigned
to the flames. In their marches, the soldiery
overloaded and injured the horses and carriages
of the peasantry, or committed shameless ex-
actions on the most flimsy pretexts. Bills of
indemnity were passed—the habeas corpus act
suspended—multitudes of Roman Catholic families driven from their homes in Ulster to
seek refuge in the wilds of Connaught, while
an armed and bigoted yeomanry were loosed
upon the country ; and the troops, sent from

England ostensibly to quell a rebellion, seemed much better qualified by their cruelty to foment it. Such is a faithful picture of the royalists and their proceedings, from 1790, until the insurrection actually broke out. Justice requires us to view the opposite party in their progress, and though it may be a painful task, yet it shall be performed with impartiality.

In times of civil commotion, it is a misfortune that any number of parties in opposition to the existing government, and whose plans and security require a secret bond of union, are too frequently identified in crime, when their present views and ultimate objects are widely though indistinctly different.

This was the case for some years prior to the eventful 1798. That savage and ruffian combination, called "Defenderism," was strangely clashed with the system of the United Irishmen. To both, the Orange party had an equal aversion; and the principles of the Reformers were blackened with the atrocities of a banditti, with whom they neither held communication, and to whose objects they neither afforded their countenance or support. The Defenders were ex-

clusively Roman Catholics of the very dregs of
society;—their leaders illiterate boors, or travelling Friars, the lowest grade of the Popish
Clergy. Plunder and assassination accompanied
their nocturnal expeditions, and their vengeance
was directed as well against the purses as the religious profession of their Protestant neighbours.

The Irish Union was composed of different
materials; and actuated by noble, though mistaken feelings, (I shall speak of it only at its
formation,) the bar, the pulpit, and the senate
gave it leaders, eminent for family and fortune,
talent and private worth; and its principles, in
1792, were the mere echo of those promulgated
by the delegates at Dungannon ten years before. The members were so numerous, as to
embrace by far the greatest portion of the opulent merchants, private gentry, and industrious
farmers in Ulster. Such was the Irish Union
in 1792; and had the Government, instead of
crusading blindly against a body which could
have been dismembered by moderation, and
conciliated by an act of common justice, entered into the spirit of the grievances so often,
so respectfully laid upon the Commons' table,

and which were read only to be rejected,—a pike would never have glittered on the heights of Tara, nor the blood of its inhabitants been spilled in the peaceful streets of Antrim !

For two years Henry pursued his studies in the University, and would have continued there until he graduated, had not a circumstance occurred which at once put a period to his sojourn, and stamped his public character for ever. In Alma Mater, politics ran as high as in any other society, and a more divided body in their political sentiments than the Fellows and Students of Trinity College, could not be found in the empire. Henry's short career was too brilliant not to throw a shade of distinction over his name. Classic and scientific honours accompanied his progress ; and, as he mixed in the athletic exercises of the Park, his superior strength and activity were noted in the field, till by a kind of spontaneous consent, the Republican party selected him for their leader.

His rival in academic glory and political sentiments, was a lad named Loftus, the orphan son of a deceased Clergyman, and the éléve of an Archbishop. His manners were plain, his temper hasty, his talents only moderate, but with industry sufficient to overcome every obstacle in his course. Next to O'Hara, Loftus was the classic hero; and although the perseverance of the latter was constantly defeated by the superior brilliancy of his gifted rival, undismayed by defeat, he redoubled his exertions, and viewed his second-rate trophies with contempt. Never were two beings more opposite:—the one, diminutive in his person, morose in his manners, and retired in his habits; the appearance of the other, dignified and noble—in temper, arch and playful—in disposition, generous, open, and convivial. The January examinations were approaching;—Loftus made prodigious efforts to surpass his opponent, and there was not an Orange Fellow in the University whose cut questions were not copiously administered. O'Hara read with his common attention, and followed his amusements in the Park. The eventful day arrived, and Loftus again found his antagonist his superior; one only hope was left—he heard that Henry had paid but little attention to the branch of science which was to form the examination of the morrow, and if he could only defeat him in it, he had every thing to hope from the noted partiality of the examiner. But when the trial came, the contest was equal, and not a shade was discernible in the answering. Such was the result of the first six hours. The victory was hollow, and Henry left the Hall amid the exultations of his friends.

When he reached Clare-street, the servant who opened the door, told him the Major was not well. " Not well! Why I was in his chamber this morning, and he was in excellent health." He ran up to his dressing-room, and found his father lying on the couch, pale and disordered. The faint smile which played on his sickly features, while he inquired after his son's success, was forced and unnatural. Henry was making anxious inquiry, when a loud knock at the door started his father, and Lord Edward's voice, in unusually high tones, asked where the Major was? and he scarcely waited for a reply till his step was heard in the passage. " Henry, my boy, leave the room. Lord Edward, not a syllable—I know it."

Henry, as he retired, looked alternately at Fitzstephen and his father. The former seemed raised almost to madness, and was labouring with a volcano of rage which O'Hara's caution barely kept from bursting. That his father and Fitzstephen were concerned in some un- pleasant affair was obvious, from the demeanour of both ; that they were not quarrelling them- selves was also plain, from the warm, though hurried greeting which had passed before him. The business must be consequential, for neither would suffer a light concern to disturb their usual tranquillity. It was almost time for him to return to the examination hall ; to leave the house in such uncertainty was intolerable ; and while he debated whether he should go to his father, and demand some elucidation of the morning's transaction, his valet placed a scroll in his hand and retired. It was Lord Edward's writing ;—

" Dear Henry—Go to your examination— make your mind easy ; at dinner you shall be made acquainted with the business you wish to know. Adieu. Victory attend you. ' Aut Cæsar, aut nullus'. Fitz."

This was Lord Edward's usual style to his favourite, and the note relieved his uncertainty. He accordingly hurried to the College; his appearance bespeaking mental ease and confidence. He observed the groups he passed loitering before the hall, eyed him with peculiar attention. The Orange party looked with something like triumph; his own friends mightily cast down. "What," thought he, "do they flatter themselves that Loftus will carry the prize off. Well, I trust I shall lower your exulting looks before long. How dull the others seem—some one has frightened them; but here's one of the gayest with a face like a mute at a funeral. Why, M'Donnell, what's the matter?—cheer up, man—you see I'm not cast down by the morning's business."

"Well, certainly Harry, you're a bold fellow: but how is your father?"

"Better, better—I left Lord Edward with him: but hark! the bell rings for victory."

All crowded into the hall; and the brilliant answering of the afternoon possessed O'Hara of both premiums.

Rage and disappointment stung Loftus to

the soul ; the decision, his heart told him, was
as it should be, but he had not temper to bear
defeat with equanimity ; with an infernal sneer,
he snatched a newspaper from a fellow-student,
and exclaimed, as he handed it over the table
to his rival, " Really your honours will be quite
a set-off against the mall mishap of your father
and his loyal confederate."

M'Donnell snatched the extended paper, and
Henry overheard, in a suppressed tone, the
words " Ungenerous——unfeeling."

The morning scene flashed on his recollection ; he demanded the newspaper. M'Donnell
refused it.   " M'Donnell, by our friendship, I
request it : *you* would not surely trifle with me.
It must be some pleasant communication that
Mr. Loftus would trouble himself to select ;"
and he bitterly eyed his pale and discomfited
opponent.   He threw his eye on the paragraph
——it ran thus——" It mus tbe a source of sincere
congratulation to every loyal and well-disposed
subject to know, that his Majesty is determined
to remove from the Army List, the names of
every favourer of Jacobites, Revolutionists,
and Rebels.   Two names of political notoriety,

for systematic opposition to the Government, will be found in this day's Gazette; and as the simple sentence, announcing their disgrace, speaks more than pages, we refer our readers to the next column." O'Hara's cheeks blazed as he rapidly ran his eyes over the paper; his sight grew dim, his brain burned as he read— " His Majesty has been pleased to direct that the names of Major Frederic O'Hara, on the retired list, and Lord Edward Fitzstephen, on the half-pay of the 19th, regiment, be erased from the Army List, for disaffection; and that these Officers be declared incapable of ever holding any commission in his Majesty's service." As Henry read, every eye was turned on him. Loftus gazed with malicious delight; while O'Hara crumpled the paper coolly in his hand, and flung it in his face. " You mean scoundrel —miserable in mind as in figure—if your wretchedness did not shield you from my resentment, this hall should not save you. As to the alleged disgrace thrown on my father and his noble friend, they despise it; they would feel degraded in serving an ill-advised King and a corrupt administration."

The noise and confusion arrested the attention of the Vice-Provost, who walked over to the table where Henry was declaiming, and who, although fully aware of the Doctor's political animosity, continued to abuse the Government with more warmth than discretion, and, in consequence, was summoned to attend the Board the following day.

The disclosure of the severe and unmerited disgrace cast upon his father and Lord Edward overwhelmed Henry with sorrow as he hurried home. The Ex-Major was astonishingly composed since morning, and endeavoured to soften the insult offered to an old and meritorious Officer. Not so Lord Edward; his feelings were vented in reproaches and threats, and the most uncomfortable day ever recollected by the parties, was heavily dragged through. The morning dawned to consummate the disgrace of the O'Haras. Henry was tried by the Board of Trinity College for sedition; found guilty of abusing the Government; condemned, and sentenced " tanquam pestis, e Collegio in perpetuo amoveri !"

Thus terminated his literary career. The

same Journals announced his classic victories and his expulsion. His father, heart-sick of Dublin, retired to his estate; Lord Edward left Ireland for Paris; and Henry bade a temporary adieu to his native land, and set out, accompanied by a gentleman of erudition and integrity, to travel wherever the disturbed state of the Continent would permit him.

———

CHAPTER IX.

With news the time's in labour.
Antony and Cleopatra.

CASTLE CARRA was now solitude itself. Another year rolled on; and while O'Hara's
mind brooded over his military disgrace, as if
to augment his chagrin, and consummate his
public degradation, a command from the Lord
Chancellor recalled his Commission of the
Peace. No impropriety could be adduced to
warrant this act of harshness, nor was any
attempted. It was briefly stated, that the
Government considered him unfit for holding
that office.

In the following paper, the death of his
gallant friend De Clifford was announced.
In a frigate of very inferior strength, he had
brought the Republican ship Egalité, of 48,
and the corvette El Corso, of 18 guns, to

close action, and after two hours' desperate
fighting, captured the corvette, and sunk the
frigate; but fell by one of the last shots from
the sinking Frenchman. His first lieutenant
caught him in his arms as he tottered. The
crew of the Endymion cheered at the moment. "Has she struck?" asked the dying
commander. "No;" was the reply, "but
she can scarcely swim. There,—there,—she's
gone, by Heaven!" "Save them!—save
them!" muttered De Clifford, and expired.

"I had almost completed my answer to
your last letter," said the Major to his son,
"when one from the widow of my gallant
friend reached me. Poor De Clifford has
named me his executor, and, with her mother,
joint guardian of his daughter. All the property he left is but trifling,—not quite two
thousand pounds; and his widow entreats me
to procure her some retired residence in my
neighbourhood. She has, I fear from necessity alone, given up her establishment; but I
am informed it will scarcely cover her debts.
The trust confided to me is truly distressing,

but it is sacred, and I shall fulfil it as I best may. I have replied to Lady Sarah De Clifford, and invited her and her daughter, on disposing of their house, to make Castle Carra their home, till they can be accommodated with a suitable residence. Therefore, my dear Harry, on receipt of this letter, I must reluctantly entreat your return. My spirits are not fit to entertain a mourner, and your presence will be necessary to perform the more active rites of hospitality.

" P. S.—I have received a reply, gratefully accepting my invitation: early in Spring I am to expect them. This will give you six months' further leave of absence. Till then, command your own time.

" F. O'H."

To connect our memoir, we will give a few extracts from the elder O'Hara's letters to his son. The notices of politics were necessarily short and cautious, as any correspondence between a suspected person, and a resident in a hostile country, would be a subject of suspicion to the Government.

" *September*, 1796.

" Politics," continued the Major to Harry,
" are alarmingly violent.   All our old neighbours are disunited.   There can be no neu-
trality in this unfortunate country.   I am an
object of suspicion to both parties.   My military disgrace has turned all the Orange faction
on my back ; and the Republicans, finding me
firm in my determination to avoid any political
connexion *at present*, eye me with something
bordering on distrust.   My retirement is now
profoundly seclusive.   When a tenant visits
the Castle on business, even his humble call
is now-a-days somewhat consequential to us.
You may remember what numbers crowded to
' his Honour for laa (law).'   The Chancellor
(and, God knows, I thank him for the measure,
though the means were not so agreeable) has
despatched my clients to justices of better re-
gulated opinions ; and when the knocker falls
at times, even poor old Pero (sole survivor
of all the spaniels) loudly testifies his astonishment.   I sometimes contrast the present
with other days.   But I have done.   Adieu."

L 2

"*October*, 1796.

" I told you, the last time I wrote, how much the society of our old neighbours was broken by the discordance of their political sentiments. You desired me to tell you how they are. I can only answer your inquiry by telling you ' they live.' Mr. Nugent has built an addition to his house, and become a violent tool of the Government. Whether his mansion has been amended in an equal ratio to his politics, I cannot pretend to say ; but I fear his fortune by both has suffered deterioration. You know my opinion of his understanding was never flattering, and I conceive him to be just a character fit for persecution, when prompted by a powerful but unprincipled aristocracy. Nugent will be the puppet, dangled by hands behind the curtain, and, in these dreadful days, may be made a terrible engine of oppression. His house is always filled with company, and rather resembles an officer's barrack than a private habitation ; and, notwithstanding its being the focus for horse, foot, and artillery, the Misses Nugent still remain unwedded.

" Of M'Cullogh I know, unwillingly, more than I do of Mr. Nugent. He, you are aware, purchased the estate of the unfortunate Fitz-maurice, and, as his new purchase stretches along the lake, parallel to the Castle Carra property, he set up a claim to Islandbeg and Islandmore. However, the islands and roy-alties of the whole lake were found to be vested in me; and his lawyer, fortunately, could make out no feasible claim, by which he might litigate their ownership. Finding his hopes of gaining those beautiful little islands by litigation desperate, he offered me 1000*l.* for them (the fellow's made of money). I returned an answer, that, in that little sa-cred spot, my ancestors, for many a genera-tion, reposed; and I would not barter the last resting-place of the O'Haras for the six thousand acres which composed the Fitzmau-rice estate. I am told he was furious, but, as he knew he dare not turn restive, like an uneasy horse, he contented himself with champ-ing on the bit a little.

" This man's extraordinary rise in life would appear fabulous, did we not know the fact to be past disbelief. His father was an orphan, and when a boy, our old herd, ' Paurick More,' (Big Pat,) remembers him for a short time in the kitchen of Castle Carra, assisting your grandfather's cook as turf-boy. He left this house, and soon after the country, for ever. Latterly, for five or six years, the name of M'Cullogh was known as a purchaser of properties in the county, and suddenly the menial's son returned. What will not money do? Every one in the neighbourhood, but the disgraced owner of Castle Carra, visited and invited the ci-devant kitchen-boy's descendant. Determined to raise a name, he is building an over-grown house, and seeking a matrimonial alliance to perpetuate it. Lord Loftus has borrowed 30,000l. from him, and actually countenanced his addresses to Lady Constantia, your old flame. Nothing, however, could bring her ladyship to listen to his detested overtures, and, they say, he is now looking after the Baronet's sister. But to have done with him, I shall sketch his appearance in the hue and cry style :—' M'Cullogh is about five feet, two inches and a half in height; round

shoulders, in-kneed, clumsy figure, much inclined to corpulency, scorbutic face, grey eyes,
and snub nose; has an awkward, shambling
walk, with a loud and vulgar manner of speaking.' Such is the lord of three estates—such
the builder of Belvue, and such the lover of
Lady Constantia Loftus!"

"*Nov.* 1796.

"I introduced Mr. M'Cullogh to you in
my last letter but one; and if you recollect
aright, I told you that I refused to let him have
the islands for love, law, or money. If you
have forgotten these circumstances, he has not;
but to the detail. We had a meeting of grand-
jurors, magistrates, and gentry, to petition parliament against the Roman Catholic claims. I
attended to oppose this measure, as I have uni-
formly done since it became the fashion to send
a yearly tirade to parliament against the *Pa-
pishes*, as these ill-starred Irishmen are called by
the yeomen who sign it. In the course of the
proceedings I spoke and dissented; the news-
papers say the speech was good; all I know
is, that it was too true. Mr. M'Cullogh,
however, was determined to give me a *dressing*

(his own words in a whisper to the sheriff), and
made a most brutal exhibition.   He poured
forth in bad English, and worse sense, a furious
libel against the Papists, and wondered how a
gentleman, who was seldom seen at church,
(meaning me) could presume to talk of matters
of religion.   I coolly replied, that I thought it
was as illiberal as impertinent in any man to
question the religious opinions of his neighbours ; as to my own part, whatever might be
defective in mine, I trusted the morality of my
character was not of a questionable complexion.
(' Hear, hear,' from friends and foes.)   I continued—' This testimony, gentlemen, is the
more grateful, as I hope it will tacitly repel
the irreligious charge brought against me by
the *honourable* gentleman,'—(strong emphasis
here.)—' I never arraigned any one for his
faith, and I never knew, nor asked, what were
the religious opinions of the high-minded gentleman opposite to me, who has dignified this
county by selecting it for his residence.   But,
gentlemen, if there be any liberality in my conduct, I inherit it from my father ; for I will be
bold in asserting that he never questioned the

tenets of the worthy gentleman's father when in earlier life he honoured Castle Carra with his presence.' All stared, and M'Cullogh grew pale as ashes. ' No, gentlemen, though my father was a rigid Calvinist, he never quarrelled with his cook for the difference of their faith ; and I have some reason to suppose, that the elder Mr. M'Cullogh occasionally accompanied that lady to the Mass-house, as in his subordinate situation the retention of her friendship must have been to him a matter of paramount import-ance.' Shall I describe the effect of this ex-posé of Mr. M'Cullogh's earlier life on himself, and on the meeting? No pen can do it. The course of the business which collected us was instantly arrested, and in the turmoil, I leisurely called my carriage, and returned to the castle. The next morning, Mr. Nugent waited on me, and after many apologies on his part, he at last informed me his embassy was seeking one.— ' An apology for telling the history of an in-teresting era in the annals of Castle Carra? That the father of the High Sheriff elect was here formerly a cook's underling ! But I must satisfy you, Mr. Nugent, as I presume you are

the plenipotentiary. Here, Philip; call Paurick More, (big Pat).' Nugent looked silly.
'Paurick,' said I, in Irish, 'was Mr. M'Cullogh and you formerly acquainted?'

'Nonough ner braig e thin, a waisther,
(there's no lie in that, master,)' said Paurick.

'What was he in my father's service?'

'Boheil beg in she kishthena,' (a little kitchen-boy.)

'Are you certain?'

'Shuraulthe a waisther,' (certain.)

'Would you swear it?'

'Thorum an lower,' (hand me the book.)

'Now, sir,' when Paurick More had left
the room, 'tell Mr. M'Cullogh that I believe
Paurick More, his father's friend's word too
firmly, to have a doubt of his real parentage
and early occupation.'

'Hem—but—hem; can I not accommodate
matters—a slight explanation—'

'Could not alter a true assertion,' said I,
with a silent bow, and rang the bell for lunch.
Nugent affirmed he never snacked, and concluded by giving me in a round-about speech,
a message for the ensuing morning. I attended,

with Mr. Drummond as my friend, on this important occasion. Mr. M'Cullogh and Nugent were dilatory in making their appearance, and at the same moment Mr. Scanlan arrived with the *posse comitatus,* and we were stayed in form from the mortal combat which we meditated. The crowd, which, from the delay, had assembled in great numbers, and either from personal affection for me, or from a feeling of disappointment in not being rewarded by an exhibition, hissed M'Cullogh and his second off the ground, and shouted forth their opinions that Mr. Scanlan was brought by my antagonist. Thus ended the affair of honour, as the public prints term it; and I presume I may henceforth, and for ever, reckon Mr. M'Cullogh among the list of my deadliest enemies."

Shortly after the receipt of this letter, and while Henry was on his return to Ireland, the long expected visiters arrived. It was evening when the Major's carriage (which had been sent to meet them at the last stage) set down at the castle. The sun was sinking in the lake, when the relict of De Clifford and her orphan daughter entered O'Hara's territory. The wild character of the scenery was calculated to impress no very flattering idea of the place of her destination on the imagination of a London lady of fashion. The road ran along the shore of the lake, and was in many places hewn out of the side of the hill, which precipitated its descent to the waters at its base. Huge masses of mountain granite here and there overhanging the travellers, threatened to crush them as they passed; and when these hills were left behind, the view only opened on a wide and lonely heath, on one side resting on the mountains, and on the other enclosed by the lough. The short and stunted copse-wood did not improve its features, and from its own declining look, added to the dreariness of the parent moor. Now and again, a few green spots of herbage were visible, and the scanty flocks which were scattered upon them harmonised in ragged poverty with the coarse pasture on which they browsed.

Before them the prospect was dreary indeed. The road apparently terminated in the lake;

and their destination was no where to be seen. Here there was a descent of half a mile, and when they turned a sharp angle, where the promontory rested its base in the waters of the lough, Castle Carra, with its antique battlements, its oaks, and its islands, burst suddenly on their view. All was improved, but not changed—the heath became less withered in its appearance, the herbage more green and frequent, the trees numerous and healthy, till at length the carriage rolled over rich meadow, beneath the shade of ancient oaks, which more immediately surrounded the mansion.

It was now almost dark. The ladies gazed on the high and gloomy pile with something like alarm; and when they stopped before the heavy entrance, every thing was done apparently to make a din—dogs barked, men scolded them in English and Irish; the hall-door was unbarred with due clangor, while the carriage-steps rattled as they fell. From the landing-place which led to the hall, the Chieftain was seen to descend, but the ladies' curiosity could not be gratified by an accurate view of his person or features. The words of welcome were

pronounced in all the warmth of Irish hospitality, by a sweet and manly voice, and with
their host in the centre, the fair visiters were
ushered into the antique hall, and thence conducted by two elderly waiting-women to their
respective chambers.

The interior of O'Hara's mansion was carefully scrutinized by the new-comers, as they
descended to the drawing-room. The staircase was but narrow, and, together with the
pannels and doors which everywhere concealed
the walls, was constructed entirely of black
oak. A few pictures and portraits in antique
framing, and indifferently painted, were suspended around, and in no way relieved the
sombre hue of the gloomy wood-work. The
ceiling was sheeted, and formed of the same
heavy timber with the massive beams on which
the rafters rested. The hall, lighted by a
small lamp, differed from the lobbies above,
only in being flagged with mountain granite ;
instead of pictures, its pannels were adorned
with hunting bugles, ancient Irish weapons,
and moose-deer horns, which had at different
times been discovered in the surrounding bogs.

A large fire, and porter's chair, occupied a corner, where two blind musicians were seated; an old man filled the seat of honour, while the huge chimney, heaped with turf, diffused heat and light around.

The drawing-room door was partly unclosed, and the ladies paused, by a kind of mutual consent, to look at the master of the house. A large and brilliant fire of bog-deal illuminated the apartment. O'Hara stood, leaning on his arm, against the lofty old-fashioned chimney-piece, and was apparently lost in meditation. His dress was deep and mournful, although in those days gentlemen, when in dinner costume, wore gay and lively colours; his height, his dark features, and raven hair, were all in unison with his melancholy mood, and the venerable air of the apartment. He was evidently a very handsome man, and although his ebon hair was here and there interspersed with grey, this uncertain indication was all which would have marked his having passed over life's meridian; his carriage was lofty and erect, and when a rustling of female dresses roused him from his reverie, the manly and unbroken step

with which he crossed the room to meet his
guests, betrayed nothing of approaching seni-
lity.   His manners accorded with his appearance—they were those of high birth and polished society ; but in his smile, although sweet
and winning, there was that shade of sorrow
mingled, which bespoke the presence of a " mind
diseased :" the efforts he made to conceal it
were, however, successful, and when the dinner was announced, the hospitality of his country seemed to have overcome every other feeling.   Lady Sarah was astonished when handed
to the dining-room ; it was spacious, and, notwithstanding its oaken pannels, magnificent ;
the furniture was heavy, but handsome ; the
plate, of which there was a profusion, ancient
and massive ; and the grey-headed butler of
O'Hara's father, with four richly-dressed footmen, were in perfect character with all.

The hall was so ample, that the entertainer
and his banquet occupied but the upper extremity ; while at the bottom of the chamber, and
scarcely visible from the table, the harpers
were seated, and according to the custom of
the country, played during the meal.   Some

curiosity was excited by the appearance of a fourth cover on the table; but an inquiry from O'Hara, "if the Doctor had returned?" partially removed it, by acquainting the ladies, that the expected was a professional gentleman. On the servant's replying that he had not, the host observed, " My friend the Doctor is nearly as eccentric in his movements as in his appearance—we never wait for him; but I hear his step; the creak of his shoe is not to be mistaken, and therefore he shall describe himself." The expected Physician accordingly entered the room with considerable bustle. He was a very little man, whose circumference far exceeded his altitude—his figure excessively *outré*—his proportions exactly those of a nine-pin, with a very rubicund countenance, which would not have brought discredit on a civic officer. Although he certainly enjoyed the advantages of a recent refit, it was easy to conjecture that the business of the toilette formed but a trifling part of the Doctor's concerns in life : his clothes were very unequally put on, no one button being fitted in its natural receptacle; the knot of his neckcloth drawn under his ear, precisely as the hangman would have placed it had he been in attendance; one cheek was obscured by hair-powder, while its fellow glistened with pomatum; his bow and introductory address were quite in character.

" My dear Doctor," said the host, when the party were seated, " we had nearly rated you an absentee—old David was active in his researches, and reported you to be missing."

" Missing," cried the Physician, " as I am to be saved, I was for the last hour in the library. Ah! poor Davy—years, years, my dear Lady, will make the best of us subject to mistakes. I remember poor Doctor Pillagrew—(here O'Hara groaned)—he died at eighty-three, and practised to the last. You may recollect Miss Golightly, Major; he gave her digitalis for a dropsy the morning she was delivered of a daughter." The Ladies looked confused, but Molloy would scarcely have remarked them had they been fainting. " On her recovery, she married a Methodist Preacher, and had a blessed death, as the man said in the funeral sermon, for she went off raising the hymn at a love-feast. Talking of death (O'Hara again groaned), I never saw a finer man on a table than poor Pillagrew; we opened him at his own request—liver scirrhous: otherwise, sound as a bell."

"For the sake of Heaven, Doctor," cried O'Hara, interrupting the reminiscences of Doctor Pillagrew and Miss Golightly, "give us some soup."

The Doctor mechanically dipped the ladle in the tureen. "Poor Pillagrew! he was a facetious man. Doctor Drench, of Edinburgh, a friend of mine, and Author of Hints on Hydrophobia—"

"Soup, soup," cried O'Hara, unmercifully interrupting anecdotes of Doctors living and dead. "Hang Doctor Drench—come, you will starve the Ladies."

The Doctor begged pardon, sent soup round the table without spoiling the cloth; and, if we except his mistaking Emily for her mother, and a fillet of veal for a roast turkey, with a few other trifling misnomers, he acquitted himself with unusual adroitness.

Nor was the first impression made by Major O'Hara on the minds of his guests weakened

M 2

by a subsequent intimacy; each succeeding day
displayed a character of bold but amiable properties, while his mental acquirements, the
fruit of much reading and reflection, enabled
him to gain an extraordinary ascendency over
the affections of his female friends. His equal
and gentle hilarity brightened the long hours,
and robbed retirement of its dulness; and, as
was sometimes the case, when the hand of care
appeared to press for a moment heavily on his
brow, some odd or mal-a-propos remark of the
Doctor, banished the cloud which hung gloom-
ily over the party, and all again was sunshine.
At times, however, his mind appeared lost in
considerations of deep moment; he often left
the drawing-room early; and Lady Sarah
De Clifford remarked, that though hours must
have elapsed after the household had retired to
rest, yet the closing of the library-door discovered that some one was still waking. Con-
ferences between O'Hara and many strangers
were frequent, and conducted with much caution, while the receipt of a letter obliged him
often to rise abruptly from the table, to which
he did not again return. Of the many visiters

of O'Hara, very few were introduced to the Ladies, and seldom any of them remained for dinner. The Castle was carefully secured at night-fall, and a person during the day was stationed on the battlements, from whence, for many miles, the view was uninterrupted.

O'Hara seemed to have much and important business to transact; and at the board, when his gaiety appeared assumed, his acting was so admirable, that none but an experienced observer could discover his mirth to be foreign to his heart. Whatever might have been his sorrows, and deeply as his concerns might occupy his mind, his politeness, or ease of manner, was never for a moment forgotten; and the Ladies could never accuse him of neglecting that which was due to his own hospitality or their sex.

The peerage told that Lady Sarah De Clifford was in her forty-third year; and but for that, and the tell-tale presence of a marriageable daughter, she might have thrown off the latter five without much fear of detection. She never had warm feelings or affections; and excepting where her own pleasure was compro-

mised, the sufferings of the nearest friend little
endangered her mental tranquillity; and to
this cold and heartless tone of character, she
might probably attribute the continuance of
fresh and unfaded beauty. She was still very
lovely; and many who were strangers to the
greater and more momentous concerns which occupied O'Hara's mind, would have pronounced
his fate and *her* victory secure. To have
achieved the conquest of his heart would have
been a desirable object from the first; but after
a longer intimacy, more than common worldly
advantage swayed Lady Sarah's conduct.
O'Hara was both amiable and handsome; and
his rank, his family, and the eclât, which even
followed him to seclusion, would have rendered
him a high object in the eyes of one to whom
penury and imprudence had made the more
elevated walks of London dissipation unattainable. However, the widow's castles were all
air-built. O'Hara's gentlemanly attention endeavoured to anticipate the wants and wishes
of Lady Sarah; but still there was no more of
warmer sentiment in this delicate and gentle
kindness, than if he had wanted eyes, or Lady

Sarah beauty. Trifling circumstances soon told the widow her chance of conquest was hopeless, and like an able general, she had scarcely broken ground, until, perceiving the fortress was impregnable, she forbore to press the siege, and retired in good time and perfect order.

Lady Sarah was a thorough manœuvrer, and finding that Castle Carra would not own her for its mistress, she determined to transfer the command to her daughter. Henry's return was, therefore, impatiently expected, and Emily was regularly prepared to entrap the young Milesian, whose subjugation was counted certain, as the lady was strictly beautiful, and the gentleman an Irishman of twenty-four.

CHAPTER X.

Sick was the sun, the owl forsook his bower,
The moon-struck prophet felt the madding hour.

Pope.

THE return of the heir of Castle Carra had been
expected for some time, and a letter, stating
that he was on his way from London, had been
received. Two years had elapsed since the
father and son had last parted, and the imagination of the parent was employed in fancying
the alteration likely to have been effected in
the manners and appearance of his absent boy.
The curiosity of the visiters was equally intense ;
they wished to see one of whose personal accomplishments every tongue was prodigal.
The minds of both were sceptical as to the
truth of the high-wrought colours with which
the name of Henry O'Hara was emblazoned.

" Could it be possible that this sequestered Castle had given birth and education to one in whose character and appearance romance might find colouring for her hero, and graces for the love-ditty of a Troubadour ?"

" Impossible," said the younger lady, with something like a sneer. " Who are these O'Hara's eulogists? That old, noisy savage, whose screams wakened us this morning, who has been (God knows how long) huntsman to the clan; he, forsooth, reckons him a prodigy, because he could ride vicious horses, and leap break-neck fences ; and then he is head of a horde of half-clad mountaineers, and knows them and their sons, and their daughters, and jabbers Irish better, I suppose, than he can speak 'English. Pshaw! I fear I shall be miserably disappointed."

" But his father," rejoined the Matron——

" Ay, Lady Sarah; but consider the difference of opportunity——the one educated in those bleak turrets with a die-away Mamma, and encircled by a collection of drunken Squires or crazy Doctors ; the other schooled in the world, and a soldier from his boyhood. Well, we

shall soon see with what justice his praises have
been trumpeted over hill and dale."

While these and such conjectures amused the
ennui of the secluded fashionables, the object
of their curiosity arrived.   It was one of those
bright and placid nights which are not unfre-
quent during the winter in Ireland.   Binnian
and Slieve Donard were capped with snow, and
contrasted their blanched summits with the dark
hue of the ridges stretched beneath their tower-
ing heights.   The night was clear and strong, and
the young moon, peeping over a little hill, shed
a gentle side-light on the lake below her.   Every
thing looked with something endearing in it to
the returning Irishman ; every heath he passed,
and every hillock his eye traced, were intimately
remembered.   When he approached nearer to
his home, each recollection became more vivid,
each feeling an agony ;—there were the towers
of his youth, and there the scenes of all his first
joys and sorrows ;—there sat his parent expecting him, and there the " mille fealtha" * waiting
to receive him.   The carriage stopped, and
leaving it to pursue its more circuitous road, he

_____
* Thousand welcomes.

took a nearer path through the plantations which skirted the Castle Park. He passed rapidly through the well-known inclosures, when turning suddenly into a little vista, he started at seeing a human figure seated on a stone, muttering, in low and hollow tones, sounds which, although not intelligible to the ear, had something in them unearthly and terrific. The light was dim, for the moonbeams were excluded by the fir-trees which surrounded this lonely dell, and superstition had not failed to seize on a spot so favourable for her traditions, and people "Glan Dullogh" with fays and spectres; an ancient barrow was its boundary, and, of course, added to the terror of this gloomy hollow. Henry O'Hara was brave, but he had some slight taint of that superstition which so generally imbues the character of the Irish of even the higher ranks. That a spot so lonely and desolate, should be chosen for the ordinary purpose of resting in, was unlikely, for the most courageous of the peasantry avoided it even in the noontide. He stood, irresolute to advance, but yet scorning to retire, while a well-known voice addressed him—" Welcome, Henry

O'Hara—Welcome! said I?   Oh! that I could
bid you one, but never did man return under
worse omens than yourself."

" In the name of God, what do you here,
Alice More?" cried O'Hara, advancing and recognising the speaker; " why sit you here, like
a night raven, to damp my happy return with
your croaking and foreboding—and how is it
that first of all I light upon you, Alice? None
count it fortunate to meet you; and never did
I see you in my father's house but in time of
sorrow and distress."

" Ask me not, Henry O'Hara, how I knew
that I should meet you—nothing earthly sent
me here—the ' Far a Knuick' (the man of the
hills) has screamed the live-long night round
the old towers—he has screamed over the place
where your forefathers are sleeping—not a hill
or valley, but has echoed with his cries."

O'Hara felt unusual alarm as he listened to
Alice More; his native gallantry of spirit, however, conquered his latent superstition, as he
boldly continued, " And what care I for the
Far a Knuick—what care I for his cries—I tell
you it is all rank superstition; you have been

deceived yourself, and you want to deceive me."

"Superstition—deceit, call you it," screamed Alice More; "I tell you, Harry, in your heart you feel a shudder. When the English broke into Shaun Rua's (Red John's) hall, and spilled his blood on his own hearth, did not the 'Far a Knuick' cry? When your grandfather expired in his bed, and none knew it, did I not hear the spirit on the hill, and was he not found cold and clammy, even when I was telling it to his serving-man? When your mother (God be good to her) died, who could sleep for the Hill-man's cries? I heard him mourning when these ill-boded English women came to the house of O'Hara; but never did his cries equal those with which he made the mountains echo for your return."

She had raised herself from the stone on which she rested, and through an opening in the trees, the moonbeams shone on her hard and heated features, and her tall form, wrapped in the loose mantle which was carelessly flung around her, recalled much of the expression given by painters to the witch of Scripture

confronting Samuel.   The uncommon energy
with which she had spoken, struck unaccountable awe into the heart of young O'Hara.
These tales were familiar to him from his childhood; and, if he disbelieved the existence of
the "Far a Knuick," he was probably the only
sceptic within the circle of many miles round
the dwelling of his family.

" Alice More," said he, " do not gloom the
hour of happiness, by anticipating what may
never be fulfilled. I fear not what may be in fu-
turity—my hour may be short and transient, but
even you, Alice, shall never make me tremble."

" Hush, hush," said Alice, placing her arm
on his, " there is a step—beware, none but
one would venture in the gloaming to the lonely
spot on which you and I are standing."

Henry's heart beat, as he strained his ear to
catch the sounds which Alice More had heard;
some one advanced, for the leaves rustled beneath a cautious footstep, and the boughs, although gently displaced, indicated that an intruder was contiguous.

" Alice," said a deep, disguised voice, " what
do you here?   Am I betrayed ; and is it mortal

man who stands beside you? Speak, or by the merciful God, I will fire at it, be it man, be it devil."

To this extraordinary address which issued from the thicket, within a few paces of the spot where they stood, Alice coolly replied, "Ungrateful boy—am I a betrayer? Need I have brought you to ' Glan Dullogh' to sell or slay you? When you lay exhausted on my own bed —when famine, fatigue, and fever made you unable to lift the cup of water to cool your burning lips, did Alice More betray you? When none could succour ye, none dare shelter ye, who, in the storm of midnight, when nothing earthly was a-foot, sought ye in the haunted cave * where the bloody Arnold murdered his grey-headed father? Pat Mahony! come forward, and see him whom you would have slain."

The person addressed sprung lightly through the bushes which had concealed him, and, with a pistol in his hand, approached confidently to O'Hara; but suddenly, with a cry of horror,

* A remarkable cavern on the Mourne coast, and the scene of a dreadful murder.

he dropped the weapon at his feet, and hid his face in his hands.

"Unhappy young man, how is it I find you? Why did I select you from all my father's people, and in the fond hope of making you comfortable to your parents and honourable to society, gave you that education which many a well-born Irishman has been denied—and what do I find you, Pat—a wandering outlaw, dragging out a detestable and precarious existence, and branded by the community as an outcast. Leave me, Pat, leave me—perhaps, in strict justice I should now give you back to the offended laws whose retribution you have for a time evaded ; but the recollection of what you once were robs me of the resolution. Leave me, Pat Mahony, and leave me for ever ; cross not my path again—retire from this country, or by the soul of my fathers, should we meet again, not even the feelings of past affection shall shelter a murderer from justice." Mahony calmly raised his head, and unbuttoned the loose grey coat which he had on ; a blunderbuss, a case of pistols, and a knife or dirk

were concealed beneath it—these he laid at his
master's feet, and then, while sobs almost stifled
his utterance, he spoke to young O'Hara—
" There, Master Henry, there ; no longer will
Pat Mahony keep the hill-side—to be called a
murderer by the world—to be the disgrace of
my father's old age was hard to bear ; but to
be scorned by you, Mister Harry—to be
thought a cold-blooded assassin—who could
bear it ! There lie, what would stretch the best
yeoman M'Cullogh could command, had he on
the heath dared to question me.   Come on, I am
ready ; good bye, Alice—heaven reward you
for what you did to me and mine ; and when I
am at the gallow's-tree, I will declare, as I did
to judge and jury, that I never, in life or death,
did injure Bryan M'Bride (God take his soul),
and as he hopes for God's mercy in the next,
(for man's in this world he neither asks nor
cares for) never did man or woman's blood lie
at the hands of Patrick Mahony !"

There was a solemnity in the appeal of the
youthful outlaw, that brought conviction to his
master's heart ; he raised him from the ground,
on which in despair he had thrown himself,

and listened to his own confession of the part
which he had acted in the tragedy of M'Bride's
murder.   He had, with others, consented to his
death, but repenting, followed the murderers
to save their victim.   He came only when
they were separating, after having accomplished
the death of the devoted informer ; he was seen
leaving the spot by a passing traveller, and on
his imperfect evidence was convicted, and sentenced to be executed.   The night preceding
the day on which he was to suffer, he made a
most extraordinary escape from the prison, and
though two hundred pounds was offered for
his detection, he evaded every attempt to seize
him.   The disaffected through the mountain
districts afforded him shelter and assistance,
and his uncommon boldness, the result of native
courage, unduly excited by desperation, spurred
him on to the achievement of many exploits,
which at once made him the admiration of the
one party, and the terror of the other.

"Ye must part, ye must part!" exclaimed
Alice; " see how the moon is rising; I will
bring you to each other soon, but ere now,
Pat Mahony, your foot should have been on

the heather of Glancullen (pointing to a high hill beside them); but God protect us—did you see any thing either of ye?"—and the cold drops stood on her high forehead.

"Nothing, Alice," said O'Hara, while Mahony cocked his blunderbuss and sprang forward.

"Lay it down, Pat—lay it down; what would arms do against a spirit—it was shorter than you, O'Hara," as she peered over his face and figure—when, turning to the outlaw, "The wraith was yours, Pat Mahony."

"Mine, Alice!" said the wanderer; "well, well," as he sighed, "the sooner I am in the ground the better. Hear me, Master Harry; perilous times are coming—blood will flow in rivers; join neither party till you see me again; you may not meet me for a time, and should I never see you more, ask Alice, and she will tell you much."

At the moment, the bugles of the cavalry sounded, and the evening gun of the garrison pealed across the lake. Alice called out loudly, "Away, not a moment must be lost!" Mahony pressed Henry's hand respectfully to his

N 2

lips, and lifting his arms, concealed them beneath his coat, and disappeared through the underwood. Alice, taking an opposite direction, beckoned Henry to follow. They passed the thick glades in profound silence, till, emerging from the coverts, they found themselves in an open avenue leading to the castle, which was now revealed in the pale moonlight. Alice paused. "O'Hara, God bless you, and may you be more lucky than all things bode you—of one thing beware—beware of love; she who will endanger your heart, is now a guest in the halls of Castle Carra; but a higher destiny awaits you—a more important object must engross your thoughts, and your country's claims predominate. Ask me no questions, I will answer none. One thing more, and I will leave you;—none have deadlier foes—none more devoted friends; but it is your fate—away, away!"

She started suddenly from his side, and before he could recover his utterance or self-possession, Alice More had turned into the coppice wood, and was no longer seen. O'Hara stood rivetted to the spot—was it a dream, or was it reality ?. This extraordinary meeting with two persons, with whom peculiar circumstances of. life and character rendered an interview so improbable, was indeed singular. Alice More was rarely seen beyond the precincts of her little garden, which, with her cottage, was placed in an unfrequented hollow between the bases of Glancullen and Binnion. That Mahony, a proscribed felon, should be at large in the evening and in a frequented park, was still more unaccountable. "But these occurrences," said Henry, "after all, do not require a supernatural solution. This strange woman, ever wayward and unsettled, would naturally choose the dark dell, as a place suited to indulge the fancies of a weak and unsteady mind ; and should I yield up my independence to the trammels of a crazy dotard ? Rouse yourself, O'Hara !—there is the home where a fond father waits to embrace you ; banish what would damp its welcome—courage!"

It was now ten o'clock, and the carriage had made its tedious circuit, and rolled over the distant avenue ; Henry rushed up the steps, and knocked loudly at the door.

" It is *his* foot," cried the blind Harper.—
" It is his knock," said old David ; and amidst
the joyous bustle of servants, and the over-
whelming caresses of his favourite dogs, Henry
rushed into the library, and was locked in the
arms of his father.

CHAPTER XI.

But I know what my own taste in female beauty is, and I will describe it. A woman five feet two inches high (without her shoes), half an inch more or less; plump, even when young, and prone to crum rather than crust as she increases in years; small-boned, small hands, and small nimble feet, and giving evident proofs that the fruit of her love is not, for want of an ample natural supply, to be banished to a hireling breast. Sprightly eyes, of I care not what colour; features that speak; a voice at once feminine and firm, and a laugh that banishes melancholy from my abode.

Cobbett.

WHEN young O'Hara retired to his chamber, he sought in vain the repose which the fatigue of his day's journey might have been expected to produce. An indistinct apprehension of danger is sometimes felt, although one cannot resolve it to any satisfactory cause; and Henry endeavoured to banish uneasy feelings which threw a feverish restlessness over his slumbers. If for a moment he succeeded in composing

himself to sleep, dreams of Mahony and Alice
More disturbed him, and he arose, to break the
chain of sombre meditations, by looking on the
placid scenery which lay before his window.
The clock struck three, and to his surprise,
voices not very distant stole on his ear; he
listened anxiously, and from a glass-door which
opened from the library upon the lawn, a man
issued, carefully muffled in a dark cloak, and
immediately the door was closed and bolted.
The stranger stopped—looked around him for
an instant, and seemed uncertain which path to
strike into. After a moment's hesitation, he
turned into a narrow walk which led circuit-
ously to the lake, and in a short time the faint
sound of his retiring footsteps ceased to be heard.
Henry hurried on his clothes, and taking his
travelling pistols from the table, passed down
to the library. All was perfectly silent, and
he found no difficulty in passing through the
same door which had given the stranger egress.
A private turn through the shrubbery led by a
neglected path directly to the water, and this
he chose as likely to enable him to overtake the
object of his curiosity. Nor was he deceived—

for on reaching the termination of the walk, cautious footsteps announced that the unknown was approaching. Concealed in the thick foliage of the Laurestinas, he perceived him issue into the moonlight, and after looking carefully round for an instant, he clapped his hands sharply—the signal was promptly answered by a small boat starting from a little inlet, and stopping at the bank to receive him. One man was in the skiff, and as Henry was about to start from his concealment and confront those mysterious persons, the well-known tones of the boatman (in whom he recognised Pat Mahony) arrested him. "Well, Colonel, what the devil kept you—three long hours—and it is so confoundedly cold."

"Was all quiet since," said the stranger.

"Still as the grave—nothing astir but ghosts and water-fowl. Was all right at the castle?"

"All," said the stranger. "Young O'Hara detained me a full hour talking of his travels to the old one, and faith I thought the father would be so new-fangled with the story, as to keep me shivering in the closet till cock-crow. I got the despatches for the Directory,

and you must land me as far up the lake as
you can."

"Come, then," replied the boatman, "let
us be moving; if M'Cullogh knew the precious
freight and crew that occupy his boat to-night,"
and he laughed heartily. "Faugh! there's as
much tawdry orange in the stern-sheets as in
the Nassau Lodge on a making-night; only it
may be useful again, by St. Peter I would stave
it, although it cost me a long hour. Here,
Colonel, here is a real Protestant oar for you,
never contaminated by a Popish paw till now—
pull away, my hearty."

The boat shot away from the shore; in a few
minutes it doubled a head-land, and Henry returned to the castle. On reaching the glass-
door, a light in his father's dressing-room attracted his attention. This apartment opened
immediately from the library, and was considered by the inmates of the house as the
private chamber of O'Hara. When engaged
here, no domestic presumed to enter, and the
task of airing and arranging it was intrusted
to his own personal attendant. Through the
opening in the shutters Henry perceived that

his father was not alone—there was another in the room, but owing to the confined aperture, the figure was but indistinctly seen ; once he passed between him and the lights, and it struck him that he had seen the person before. At the moment, his father lifted a taper from the table, as about to retire, and he was obliged to pass hastily into the library. Before he reached his chamber, the noise of the locking of the door indicated that O'Hara had retired for the night.

Once more he threw himself upon a restless bed—fancy was too busy to let him sleep, and the suspicion long entertained was too true—his father was an *United Irishman !* Every circumstance confirmed it—the characters he had remembered as intimates at Castle Carra were notoriously inimical to the existing government, and would his father hold sentiments different from his associates ? No—he knew that the recollection of his military disgrace rankled deeply in his breast—his character as a soldier, and his popularity with the disaffected, would render him a desirable leader to head the existing conspiracy ; the offer would be made, and the remembrance of what he considered as the persecution of the Irish executive would stimulate him to accept this dangerous honour, and thus display political feeling and gratify private revenge.   Yet if his father was so deeply concerned as he had reason to suspect he was in the conspiracy, how should it happen that he was permitted to remain at large, while the other reformers were prisoners or exiles; and when Lord Edward, his associate and friend, was obliged to conceal himself in the country, or remain beyond seas ? On the cool, calculating temper of his father he relied much ; but the insult offered to the honour of a jealous soldier by the government, was too keen to be forgotten, and would spur a duller spirit to retaliation.   These reflections robbed him of his rest, and the night of his return was the most unhappy he had ever passed beneath his paternal roof.

The same anxiety which had kept him from repose made him an early riser, and he strolled into the Park to enjoy the freshness of the morning air.   None of the family were stirring —the domestics were engaged in their custo-

mary occupations, and the wolf-dogs deserted
the guardianship of the Castle-hall to ramble
with their young master. A Danish Fort was
at the other side of the gardens, and, from the
summit of its grassy mound, commanded a
noble prospect of all the variety of scenery
which Castle Carra boasted. How often had
he laid himself upon its shelving sides, and read
and mused away the hours, before manhood,
and its inseparable anxieties, had chased the gay
and happy visions of thoughtless childhood.
Seated on the bank, over the tops of the surrounding evergreens, he contemplated two striking objects, and each brought its reflections.
The little island where his ancestors for many a
generation slept, lay before him—the lake was
unruffled by a wave, excepting where the trout
sprang at the passing insect, and broke its sur-
face here and there with many a circling eddy.
The stillness of the water, the dark foliage of
the fir and cypress trees, which grew on the in-
sulated Burying-place, recalled the memory of
her who rested beneath their gloomy shade ;
he thought of " years agone," when she had
rambled with him over the adjacent grounds,

and his eye was now " upon the very spot—
the last to which his feet had followed her."
The tear of filial sorrow trembled on his cheek ;
but, when his glance rested on the livelier objects which lay beyond the water, the soft emotion vanished ; and, as he dashed the tear away,
the darkened brow and flashing countenance
betrayed the presence of some unwelcome object ;—it was the large and magnificent mansion
of M'Cullogh ; every thing connected with it
bespoke the wealth and profusion of the owner
—an immense park was newly walled in, spacious gardens were laid out, while plantations
of prodigious extent encompassed this princely
demesne.   " And was it not enough," thought
he, " to heap on the house of O'Hara every
insult which political rancour could inflict !
Was it not enough to place our name in the
mouth of every brawling bigot, but this upstart must come to beard us at our door, and
presume to bribe us for a spot sacred to our
ancient family—a pleasure-house above my
mother's tomb !—her ashes to be violated by a
menial ! "

It was, indeed, a bitter moment ; the insulted

honour of a high-born Irishman was excited,
and the softer sympathies a mother's memory
had recalled, only gave deeper poignancy to
feelings outraged by an arrogant intruder.
Footsteps were heard, and he perceived two
females approaching—their appearance could
not be mistaken—and Lady Sarah De Clifford
and her daughter stopped nearly beneath the
mound he stood upon.   The elder and taller of
the two was still a fine woman ; and confident
that the charms she had once so lavishly possessed were but slightly impaired by the hand
of time, appeared, by the studied elegance of
her dress, determined still to assert her claim
to admiration.   Her face was of that order
which never fails to command attention from
even the most careless admirer of beauty—the
features were marked and regular, the eye full
and brilliant ; but a haughty assumption of
superiority was discernible in every look, and
an unconscious knitting of the dark and arching
brow, betrayed a temper impatient of contra-
diction and intolerant of restraint.   Henry
turned his attention to the younger lady ; never,
he determined, had he seen so lovely a face,

never had he viewed a more perfect form. She
seemed fuller in person than females usually
are at that early period of life ; but a total absence of every thing coarse and inelegant gave
to the roundness of her figure that rich and
sumptuous character with which statuaries
have gifted their Hebe and Sleeping Venus.
The form of her bosom and arms was exquisite ;
and when she stooped to tie her sandal, which
had by accident been unfastened, a foot and
limb of perfect symmetry were disclosed : the
shape of the face was particularly fine—the
fairness of the complexion strikingly contrasted
with nut-brown hair, 'while the wreathed smile'
which curled on the lip, and lightened in the
eye, gave that life to loveliness without which
even beauty cannot charm.

" Well, I never supposed such cruelty ex-
isted in this wicked world—to think that people could exist four long hours in a room of
West Indian temperature ! Country routes and
strong tea would destroy me in one winter ; and
that noisy mob at loo and the whist-table, was
enough to destroy the nerves of Broughton
himself.   How I pitied you, Mamma, after I

was tired pitying myself. ' Lady Sarah, (mimicking) ogh! if you had but another *trumph,* and I had the king, and you had the queen, and he had the ten, and she the knave, why we would have been game. Well, we'll squeeze their dollar after all, I hope.'"

" Emily, for the sake of Heaven, never name that beastly Scanlan to me—the brute knows no more of whist than magic; and then to have him drawling out after every deal his *ifs* and *ands,* till half the pack are disposed of; and the savage is half an hour what he calls ' putting them on their legs ;' he would no more attempt to play with a knave, heels uppermost, than with his eyes shut."

" And the dancing," continued the young lady ; " the musicians drunk, the kitchen emptied to the very turnspit to see the quality, the low room reeking with mutton lights—why, my ottar had no more effect over this combination of villanous smells than dead lavendar or withered rose-leaves. But where is the Star —the Phœnix—the Apollo Belvidere—the Nonpareil. Oh! Lady Sarah, I am dying to meet this eighth wonder.   Bell, luckiest of waiting-women, has seen him, and pronounces him an Adonis proper, of six feet two inches."

Henry began to feel a little uneasy; he was an unintentional listener, and there would be now much awkwardness in a discovery.   The dogs at the moment rustled through the under-wood.   "Some one is coming this way," said Lady Sarah.   "Let us strike into the other walk."   Emily threw her shawl round her shoulders, and turning away, left young O'Hara in undisturbed indulgence of his own thoughts. How long his musings would have continued, we cannot pretend to guess, for the breakfast-bell startled him from his reverie.

"Have you seen my truant boy," said O'Hara, as he entered the breakfast-room. "But no——his first visit will be to. the kennel or paddock, where his old favourites are placed in honourable retirement.   We never part with our horses, Lady Sarah; when they have lost their vigour in our service, we allow them food, shelter, and protection; and, among yonder group of venerable hunters, (which he pointed out in a distant enclosure) you may remark two milk-white ponies, one was the first horse which carried Henry when a child, and the other the last favourite of his lamented mother. What a brute Scanlan appeared to be, when he recommended me to shoot them, or remove them to the heaths of Finlough, as their pasturage would fatten beeves admirably. Poor animals! The first was a merciful proposition, when compared with the last. But here comes my boy," and his eyes brightened as he gazed on the form that entered ; " here comes the heir to all the pride and poverty of Castle Carra!"

After the ceremonial of introduction was over, and the business of the breakfast-table permitted a furtive glance to be interchanged between the ladies, Lady Sarah's eye reproached her daughter with incredulity, while the heightened colour on Emily's cheek confessed how truly fame had spoken, when she boasted of this accomplished cavalier.

The Doctor's vacant chair produced an inquiry from Henry, where his old friend was ?

" Really, Mr. O'Hara," said Lady Sarah,

" that is a question of some difficulty. I exhibited him in more than usual health and spirits at Mr. Nugent's, last night, but having repeatedly inquired for my Cicisbeo, when the carriage was ordered, I discovered that I had been cruelly abandoned by the false knight, who had been seen riding off with a countryman, but whether on a physical or political errand, no person could pretend to determine."

" I'll acquit him of the latter, unless he is marvellously changed since I left Ireland."

" But here," said the Major, " comes a courier, and probably brings tidings of the lost gallant ;" and, as he looked again—" Himself, by all that's healing !"

Doctor Molloy had been called from the rout of the preceding evening, to attend a sick tenant of Castle Carra, and having been detained to a late hour beside the patient's bed, had taken up his abode for the night with an adjoining farmer. Here the news of his favourite's return had reached him at the moment he was venting his wrath on the Village Apothecary. To roar for his pony, and strike into a lame canter, was the work of a moment; and, when discovered from the windows, he was evidently in violent emotion; while a peasant, without hat or shoes, was running alongside. A discharge of technicals announced their nearer approach—

"Sinner that I am, I tell you it was no more Socotrine than Asafœtida. What will the world come to? Nothing but Jamaica, vile Jamaica; but where's Harry—where's Harry? I say, you Hobson, tell Fillup to 'tere et divide in charte;' but zounds, why talk to a clod-hopper. I'll write."

"Af your Honour would write plain, for the other Doctor says he can't read it—"

"The other Doctor, he's no Doctor—an Apothecary, Pharmacopolist, adulterator of aloes. Ah! Harry, I see you—Damn Fillup, sells Jamaica, and calls it Socotrine." The Doctor's joy at his Pupil's return was indescribable. "Never thought to see you home—hate the French,—Goths, Barbarians. Cut off Lavoisier's head—first Chemist in the world;—tucked up the Sieur Fredaine to a lamp-iron—unequalled in comparative anatomy."

Molloy swallowed a hasty meal, and followed his Pupil out, to ascertain if he had really escaped from those ruthless Republicans, who showed so little respect to Chemists and comparative Anatomy.

CHAPTER XII.

—————————And then the Justice

*   *   *   *   *   *

Full of wise saws and modern instances.

As You Like It.

Time flew rapidly—nothing of consequence occurred at Castle Carra—the days 'passed in receiving the visits and congratulations of the
neighbouring gentry, and to the surprise of
the O'Haras, and joy of Lady Sarah, many
families whom political opinions had prevented
for a long time from calling at the Castle,
seized on the return of the heir as a proper
opportunity of leaving their names, and thus
renewing a former intimacy. In revisiting his
ancient haunts, Emily generally accompanied
young O'Hara; and the constant business which
engrossed the Major's time, and Lady Sarah's
indolence, left them, of necessity, much toge-

ther.   An invitation to a party at Mrs. Glossins, reminded Henry that he had not returned
the visits of his friends, and he mounted his
horse and set out to make a round of the neighbouring mansions.

The first visit of the morning, was to his next
neighbour, the Justice.   Mr. Scanlan had been
for many years the proprietor of a country
shop, in which he had carried on trade to some
advantage, when the death of a maiden aunt
induced him to leave off business, and retire to
a profitable farm, which had been the property
of the departed virgin.   Fortune took one pair
of scales out of his hands only to replace them
with another ; for at the next contested election the Government candidate, in consideration of the use, *pro tempore*, of certain forty-
shilling freeholders, procured him the commission of the peace, and conceded the balance of
justice to his custody.   In the country for many
miles round, there were few less exceptionable
Magistrates—he jobbed, and so did they all ;
and then he was an empty, but a good-natured,
fool. The Quarter Sessions heard his harangues,
but never blushed for his persecutions.   In his

office he talked plaintiff and traverser tired of
law ; and as he always, instead of encouraging
them to hostilities, endeavoured to persuade
them to peace, the going Judges had seldom
any of his handy-work to distract them at the
Assizes. He himself was the only sufferer, for
he was laughed at by the aristocracy, and
humbugged by the mob.

Through a long winding lane, darkened by
high quickset hedges, Henry approached the
mansion. It was an old-fashioned building, in
which taste and cleanliness never seemed to
have been on terms of intimacy. On arriving
by a circuit through piggeries and cow-sheds,
and turf-stacks at the grand entrance, his loud
knock brought a wild-looking, staring lad to
the door, and the following colloquy ensued:—

" Pray is your master at home ?"

" He is, or he's all as one—"

" You're a liar," roared an old woman,
starting out from the kitchen; " and ye know
ye are, Paddy Pheahen." The accused turned
wrathfully round.

" I tell you, Molly Corr, that his Worship
is at home, af ye'd but tell God's truth."

" But he's not, ye whalp, ye," returned Molly Corr.

" Bad luck to the liars !" ejaculated Master Pheahen.

" Isn't that the taxman, ye baste, ye ?" cried the old lady, in no suppressed whisper, as she bolted forward.

" No, it's not, ye ould Ommadawn * !" shouted the boy. " Don't I know him well, a wee, hard-featured man, on a sorrel mare."

Henry hearing himself taken for one of not the most popular professions in Ireland, announced his name. The old woman curtsied to the ground, while the footman jumped out of the door.

" His worship's, please your honour, in the mud, (turf-bog). Run, Paddy Pheahen, the devil's luck to ye, and tell him who's come to see him." Molly then hooked O'Hara's horse at the door, and ushered him into the mansion.

During the absence of the proprietor, Henry amused himself by examining the apartment. It was evidently the chamber of audience into which he had been conducted. *The Justice's*

* *Ommadawn* or *Omadaun*, in Irish, means *a fool.*

Assistant was open on the table, among paper
and implements of writing. The library con-
sisted of a dozen or two of old and odd volumes,
most probably procured on easy terms from
some itinerant bibliopolist since the elevation
of the enlightened owner. A fowling-piece,
fishing-rod, and dog-couples, were suspended
above the chimney-piece. On the opposite
wall, and exhibited to the very best advantage,
hung the military accoutrements of his honour,
who was first lieutenant in the Cultimaugh
Cavalry; while boots, breeches, and all sorts
of garments, occupied sundry pegs in the
apartment. This chamber seemed also to be
the refectory of the mansion, for the table was
covered with the necessary apparatus for eating,
and a tea-kettle simmering on the fire, associated with a black bottle and sugar-bowl, inti-
mated that Justices of the Peace were, like other
mortals, liable to occasional thirstiness.

The visit of the young stranger seemed to
have created a mighty confusion throughout
the edifice—loud and earnest whisperings were
heard in the hall—at last the door burst open,
and in rushed Paddy Pheahen; he flew to a

press, but exclaiming—" Holy Bridget! the more ye haste, the worse ye'll speed," disappeared ; but soon returned with a fork, with which he attacked the door of the cupboard, dashed it violently open, and from this repository extracted the usual implements for shaving—applied the box to the pipe of the teakettle, and proceeded in raising a lather with due diligence. Henry stared with amazement at the oddity of the scene, when Pat with great composure requested that " as his Honour was brave and lengthy, he would lift him down the leathers."

The boon was granted. Pat threw the breeches across his arm, tore down a pair of top-boots from a peg, and exclaiming, " The Justice will be with you in a shake," bolted out of the apartment.

After a considerable delay, Mr. Scanlan, fully attired, entered, and with respect and cordiality welcomed the visiter to his house, and congratulated him on his improved and altered appearance. He protested he never had a more constant and punctual customer, he meant friend, than his father, and concluded his speech by entreating him to take pot-luck, in a *bachelor's way*, with him on Tuesday. Henry accepted the invitation, and after a few desultory observations on the game-laws, and the advantage of planting potatoes in drills, instead of riggs (ridges), the visiter took leave of the magistrate, and rode slowly from the door.

Rockland, the seat of his friend "the Captain," (as Mr. Nugent was called by the country people) lay on the opposite side of Ballycarnaney (the name of Mr. Scanlan's chateau.) It was necessary to pass by the Justice's hay-yard to reach the cross-road leading to the commander's, and from an enclosure the voice of Pat Pheahen was heard singing with great spirit, although his notes were frequently lost among the screams of alarmed poultry. Pat was too intent on his music and the business which then occupied him, to perceive that he was not alone; he held a hen in his grasp, and from the attitude of the bird and the presence of a knife, Henry conjectured that deliberate murder was about to ensue. Pat, all unmoved, sang gaily on—

> My love, says I, you're Venus fair—
> No, sir, says she, I'm Norah Creena.

When the voice of Molly Corr arrested the
harmony. "Drap her, Pat Pheahen, drap
her; he'll not stop, thank God, for dinner.
Agh! if we were but over Tuesday; and its
the yalla hin that's sittin, ye have a hauld of.
Oh, ye natarel!"

Pat Pheahen flung the hen at Molly Corr,
bid the devil bother her for an ould ———: the
monosyllable was luckily lost in the confusion,
and as it probably might not have been flattering to Mrs. Corr's character, we will omit con-
jecturing what the epithet was. Pat clapped
his hands in his pockets, whistled a loud and
lively air, and danced gaily to his own music.

Rockland at a little distance appeared to
have been formerly insular; a flat marshy
country, in many places covered with water,
surrounded it on every side. The eminence
arising from those morasses, on which the house
stood, had for a century back been the residence of the Nugents, and yet it was but im-
perfectly reclaimed. When Henry had last
been in the country, Mr. Nugent was commencing a large addition to the mansion, and
he had afterwards understood that this, added
to his former embarrassments, had severely

injured the 'Squire's property, already loaded
with incumbrances. As he approached Rockland, every thing looked as it had always done.
The entrance-gate was off its hinges, and many
practicable breaches were visible in the park-
wall, but the present appearance of the mansion was most singular: it was what an Irish
artist would term of the true " Composite
order ;" for, being the handywork of several
of the Captain's progenitors, each man seemed
merely to have consulted his own taste, un-
prejudiced by that of his predecessor. The
wings and additions were as different as they
were numerous—some were built of brick,
others were constructed of stone. The interior
was still more curious ; for the numerous additions had their several lobbies and staircases,
and to reach some of the " Wee-set-offs," (as
the domestics of the family entitled these out-
shots,) short turns, ascents and descents, were
so numerous, that the whole edifice seemed to
be built pretty nearly on the plan of the Cretan
Labyrinth.

A person who acted as porter joined Henry
at the gate, and accompanied him to the man-

sion.   Two men, who at his first entrance into
the avenue had come forward to the front of
the house, now disappeared.   Their showy
dresses and arms, however, caught Henry's
eye, and he inquired of his companion who
they were?   The fellow looked knowingly on
hearing the question, and replied in an under
tone—

"The Captain, please your Honour's, on his
keepin, and its two of the yeomen, who're
watching for fear of bailiffs."

"Good Heaven!" observed the visiter, "is
it possible that a man in that embarrassed situation would think of seeing company, and his
house beset by creditors?"

"Arrah the devil a man of them dare come
there," replied the gate-keeper, "for two
clainer or sharper boys aint in the corps than
the two very boys that's gardin him, and a
whistle would bring the dogs from the yard
and the boys from the kitchen."

Perhaps it was the intimate terms on which
the janitor and horseman appeared to be, or
probably from a prior knowledge of the visiter
being expected, which prevented these tutelary

Genii from barring his passage; on the contrary, one of them advanced from his ambus-
cade, and having received O'Hara's horse,
applied his knuckle to his mouth, and whistled
loudly. A boy answered the signal by coming
to lead the steed to the stable, and Henry
stepped into the hall.

He entered the mansion unannounced, for the
gate-keeper, acting as a vidette, immediately returned to his post, and the soldier as quickly absconded. A knocker would have been desirable,
but the door unhappily proved to be unfurnished
with that customary appendage. No servant
was visible, and no bell appeared by which one
could be summoned. Repeated bursts of merriment were heard from the apartment on the
right, and Henry determined to enter this
joyous assembly. He paused with his hand on
the lock—romping, he knew, was the order of
the day at Rockland, but the noise and tumult
in the drawing-room was most tremendous.
Feeling, however, that if any of the inmates
discovered him as he stood, he might be suspected to be a listener, he boldly pushed the
door open. The entrance was not undisputed,

a chair-cushion, hurled with mighty force,
struck the wall beside him, and narrowly
missed his head.   Henry started back at receiving this extraordinary salutation, while the
females of the party, discovering that a stranger
had entered, uttered a wild scream, and ran to
sofas and chairs, leaving the carpet strewn
with cushions, gloves, and bonnets.   A handsome young man in regimentals advanced from
the head of the room, and apologized for his
great apparent rudeness, " but really he
thought that Mr. Edward Nugent, who had
just left the room, had been returning." Henry
smiled at his mistake, and assured him that no
apology was necessary, and, addressing himself
to Miss Nugent, who was covered with blushes
in the corner, renewed his former acquaintance,
and begged not to be considered a stranger.
The easy, volatile manner of the speaker had
more effect than his words; he was speedily
introduced and acquainted with all the party.
Familiarity gradually ensued—romping recom-
menced by degrees, and in five minutes from the
date of his debut, Henry was on the floor an
active combatant.

CHAPTER XIII.

The devil take order, now! I'll to the throng.
Henry V.

THE latest addition to the neighbourhood we mentioned, was Mr. George Glossin, late of Grafton-street, Dublin, who had by great industry and good leather, made a fortune as a ladies' shoemaker. His lady was a professed ' Bas Bleu,' and had formerly obtained some celebrity as a provincial performer, before Mr. Glossin led her from the Temple of Thespis to the Altar of Hymen. When the Fitzmaurice estate came to the hammer, he purchased, by order of his lady, a small hunting-lodge, as Mrs. Glossin was ambitious to lead a life of classic retirement. She changed the name from Tallyho to Pompeii, demolished dog-kennels without mercy, and new modelled the Villa to her own perfect satisfaction. Mr. Glossin was

P 2

what ladies call an excellent family man ; he
was most submissive to his wife, and never ven-
tured to think or act without previously obtaining the approbation of his gifted helpmate.
A ride on his fat dun pony, a bottle of wine
after dinner, and permission to sleep *ad libitum*,
rendered him the happiest of mortals. He
never interfered with politics, although Mrs.
Glossin was a staunch Republican ; and, as he
was clearly unfitted for active life, neither party
troubled him on the subject.

Major O'Hara had gone through the form
of visiting and entertaining the Glossins on
their arrival in the country, but as he rarely
went into company, their acquaintance had almost ceased. On the arrival, however, of Lady
Sarah at Castle Carra, Mrs. Glossin was
among the first to visit one whose name had
been so often recorded in the annals of tonnish
life ; and the day after Henry's return was
known, Mr. Glossin and his dun pony were
put in requisition to invite him to what his
Lady called " her Literary Melange." What
kind of concerns Mrs. Glossin and her Melange were, young O'Hara could not imagine.

His father knew nothing of them; Lady Sarah could only tell that she heard that Glossin had been a shoemaker. Dr. Molloy, who had been there professionally, assured him that he was in a state of dotage, and the remainder of the family perfectly deranged. The Doctor protested to God, nothing but the wish he ever had to disseminate useful information, would tempt him to have any fellowship or intercourse with Miss Carney, who resided with Mrs. Glossin, and whom he pronounced to be a vain and impudent maniac. She had the hardihood to assert, that painting was a nobler art than physic; however, he would this once deign to tolerate her, but never, never, would he have a good opinion of any woman who would compare a dauber of canvass with a Professor of Pharmacy. What would Davy Drench say if he heard her?

Henry's curiosity was much excited to see this extraordinary family; some unexpected guests had dined at Castle Carra, and it was consequently late when the party arrived at Pompeii. During the momentary stop in the entrance-hall, while the ladies were unshawling,

a most extraordinary uproar was heard in the
reception-rooms, and the parties paused by
mutual consent, as a violent quarrel was then
raging between Doctor Molloy and a number
of the gentler sex.

" Oh! laws, Doctor, dear, there's Mrs.
Moneypenny, and she in her present delicate
situation;"—" and Mrs. Jordan," cried another damsel;—" and Mrs. Dowdale," said a
third; " Ladies, for God's sake—;" but another volley of voices overwhelmed the speaker.

" You, Doctor, who know the consequences;
why Mrs. Black's as white as a sheet." " Salts
for Mrs. Dowdale," shouted another. " Don't
be alarmed, Mrs. Jordan, he would not be so
cruel at to read that dreadful paper." " Will
you hear me, ladies?" A still more terrific
burst totally overpowered the unfortunate
Doctor, and the servant seizing on a moment's
calm, at the full strength of his lungs announced " Lady Sarah De Clifford."

The reception rooms of Pompeii were
crowded to suffocation, as the country had
risen *en masse*, attracted by the novelty of a
literary display. The entré of the Castle Carra

party seemed electric. Lady Sarah's rank and jewels, and Emily's beauty combined, were certainly enough to derange the order of a country rout. One party flocked to gaze upon the lovely stranger, and another to welcome young O'Hara. From the moment they entered, Mrs. Glossin appeared to forget that her rooms contained any persons save themselves, and even the High Sheriff was for a time unlooked; but " malgré" all her efforts, the hostess found monopoly impossible, till at last she cunningly contrived to place them in a corner, and occupy a chair which commanded the devoted group.

" Pardon me, dear Mr. O'Hara, but really the uncommon satisfaction I feel in having such an addition to the little circle of Pompeii has flurried me excessively. Beauty and Genius should ever go together," as she glanced right and left. " Dr. Molloy has been loud in your praises—I mean your mental; but I have forgotten you;—here, Joanna, (to a little girl, her daughter,) send the footman with coffee. I call Joanna after the pride of Genius and of Women, Joanna Baillie. James, the tray. Mr.

Glossin's mother and I quarrelled on the subject : a good, plain sort of body, but not a ray about her ! She entreated me to call her Deborah, and tendered a five hundred pound debenture as a douceur, but I scorned the vulgar bribe, and Deborah and her detestable debenture were discarded from my nomenclature—and there she is ' without a shilling, but a nobler name,' as Miss Carney sweetly expressed it in a delightful little poem, elicited by the occurrence. Here, Mirabeau, (to an amazingly ugly little boy) call George Washington. Poor Charlotte Smith has burned her foot, and my little Bonaparte is quite an infant, ' mewling and puking in his nurse's arms,' as the immortal Bard has it. George Washington, as you may perceive, has suffered from the small-pox ; but, thank Heaven, Genius is not subjected to the calamities incident to beauty ; and though Pope was plain, who captivated so many hearts ? But, my dear Mr. O'Hara, will you, for Heaven's sake, endeavour to pacify the Doctor, and we shall have our second reading." And, indeed, a pacificator was necessary, as the Doctor furiously resented the treatment his fasciculus (as he termed his morceau) had received, which having been assailed with a charge of indecency, was (as Bob Acres would say) "voted incapable."

No one could have undertaken the task of soothing the irritated author, with any probability of success, but Henry, who having taken him aside, persuaded him that so ingenious and erudite an affair as the aforesaid fasciculus, was quite above the standard of female understanding; lamenting, at the same time, the mental weakness of the sex, and whispering the old proverb of "Pearls thrown to swine." The Doctor was mollified, and Miss Carney was called on for her contribution.

Miss Carney, the dear friend and literary companion of Mrs. Glossin, was known to the world as the Authoress of two or three successful Novels, and a volume of Namby Pambys, of the Della Crusca school. The friendship subsisting between the Lady of Pompeii and the Novelist was most singular—for whether from her manners, in which a more than ordinary share of acid prevailed, or some nameless cause, the women generally disliked her;

while, with the other sex, she was still more
unfortunate, for the men usually concluded the
description of some unlucky female by saying
she was "just such another devil as Miss Carney." Her personal appearance was not in
her favour—she was tall, thin, and angular ;
and having reached that unhappy period of life
when it is said unwedded ladies all but despair,
the strange efforts she made use of to repair
the damages of time, by dress and the "art
cosmetique," placed her in that order of beings
which in Ireland are distinguished by the title
of *Dusts*. . On this eventful evening she was
attired in the very extremity of a freshly-im-
ported fashion ; her hair wreathed fancifully
with oak-leaves and flowers—roses she had in
profusion, but they were confined to her head,
for those which had erst bloomed upon her
cheek, had absconded before the recollections
of the greater part of the company could recall the memory of their existence.

Miss Carney advanced with due dignity to
the table. The company were as quiet as
could be expected, as the females were half
tired, and the men half drunk. She surveyed

her auditory with a gracious smile, and unclosing a huge portfeuille, commenced her prefatory address :—

" The short and trifling scene I am about to confide to your indulgence, is from the MS. Romance of ' The Awful Monitor, or the Caverns of St. Antonio.' The characters which will be introduced are, the Duca D'Urbino ; Rosalvina dell' Angelicano; Annette, her Maid ; the Viscounts Manfredonia, Squanderini, and Martelli ; their profligate companions, Signors Contarino, Marinelli, and Scamparoni ; with the Bravoes Sanguinario and Spado ; the Castellan, Apothecary, Confessor, Sbirri, Gondoliris, and a part of the Banditti."

" Lord preserve us from such a brigade," cried a Yeomanry Officer. " Amen," was generally responded.

Miss Carney requested the candles should be snuffed, and then smilingly commenced—

" Night came on dark and dismally—the clouds, in thick and eddying columns, densely shaded the lofty watch-turrets of the Castello, while vivid lightning, accompanied by pealing thunder, awfully illuminated its dusky corri-

dors; the demon of the storm bestrode the
blast, and yet, amid the pauses of the tempest,
bursts of noisy merriment ascended from the
grand saloon, where D'Urbino revelled with
his profligate compeers. One bosom in the
Castle was undismayed, for conscious innocence
cheered it. Oh! that was Rosalvina's. 'Alas!'
sighed the sufferer, ' what a night is this for
the guilty. Does not thy flinty bosom tremble,
Duca D'Urbino?'

"The sufferer's soliloquy was interrupted by
a noise, and a firm and sounding step approaching the painted chamber, resounded along the
tesselated passage. The unknown stopped and
knocked loudly at the door,—the sound was instantly repeated, and before our fainting Heroine could say ' Come in,' the portal was
rudely unclosed, and the ruthless Sanguinario
entered.

" Rosalvina sprang from the sofa, and with in-
dignant displeasure pourtrayed in her fine face,
demanded, ' Who was the mannerless intruder?'

" ' Donna,' replied the unblushing Bandit,
' it is Sanguinario, your Excellenza's very
humble slave, who now intrudes on your Serene
Highness, to conduct you to the expiring Duca.'

" Indignation gave way to terror, as with ashy paleness tinting her lovely features, Rosalvina gasped, ' Merciful Heaven! is he dying ?'

"' Only with love,' said the Robber, elevating his whiskered lip into a demoniac grin.

"' I will not go,' said the trembler ; ' the daughter of Angelicano holds no intercourse with inebriate Cavaliers.'

"' And this is then your resolve, haughty Donna.'

"' It is, man of blood,' replied the persecuted Contessa.

"' Ha!' roared Sanguinario, as he paused for a moment, and gazed on her with a look of indescribable malice, ' this shall be remembered;' and flinging the door almost off its hinges, he strode furiously from the apartment.

" Scarcely had the Bandit retired, leaving our Heroine in a state of pitiable agitation, when the light-hearted Annette entered ; but on perceiving the pallid countenance of her angelic mistress, the attached creature burst into tears, and exclaimed, ' Oh! has that terrible Sanguinario been here ?'

" ' He has,' faintly articulated Rosalvina.

" ' Oh! did you but know what has happened since I left your Excellenza, to get hartshorn from the new Apothecary, Pedrillo; you may know him, Donna,—he wears a sooty-coloured wig, and has a turn in his left eye—',

" ' Go on, dear Annette, and never mind Pedrillo's left eye,' said Rosalvina, with a heavenly smile.

" ' Well, thank the Virgin, I have got the hartshorn, or you would faint past recovery. Well, as I was crossing the west corridor, to reach the spiral staircase, leading to northeast gallery, I heard a footstep rapidly following me; blessed Mary, how my heart palpitated; I could neither go back nor forward; but do not look so pale, dear Donna. On came the person, and who do you think it was?'

" ' Probably Anselmo, the gardener,' said the Heroine.

" ' Oh, no, poor man, he has been confined in the dungeons for the last week, by order of the Duca, for being accessory to a bad sallad, although he offered to take his oath the fault lay in the dressing—'

" ' Well, well, go on, Annette.'

" ' It was Ludovico,' said the Waiting-maid, casting down her eyes and blushing."

" Damn'd thrash, damn'd thrash," muttered Doctor Molloy, loud enough, unfortunately, to be heard by the Authoress, who flung down the MS. and with fury flashing from her eyes, attacked the inconsiderate Physician.

" Such trash is it as your clinical catch-penny, or cases, or whatever name you gave your abominable account of a——"

" Oh! fie, Miss Carney," exclaimed half a dozen Misses.

" Ladies, I stand corrected ; his obscene book will not bear quotation."

" My obscene book!" shouted the Doctor. " What was your last novel about, Miss Carney? Worse before God than a county calendar, all rape and robbery." Both parties advanced in a threatening attitude. " The old man's case!" shouted the Novelist.

" Viola's mother in the bower!" roared the Doctor.

The young woman screamed " Romance !"

" Theodora ruined by Ferdinand!" sputtered
Physic.

What would have been the consequence it is
impossible to conjecture, had not a servant at
this critical moment called out—" Supper's
served."

Every person was immediately on the alert ;
some shouted, supper !—some cried, damn the
Duca !—and others, damn the Doctor ! While
Miss Carney and the author of " Clinical
Cases" were borne off by the crowd, heartily
abusing each other, until their voices were
lost in the " Mêlée" for seats at the supper
table.

" Well, really I could not have imagined
such a scene as Mrs. Glossin's melange made,"
said Lady Sarah, as the carriage started from
Pompeii.

" Yes," replied O'Hara; " the early part of
the concern was unequalled—that execrable
Novellist—I wish she was in the hands of her
own banditti, or in the deepest dungeon of her
friend Duca Urbino, or whatever name she
gave the gentleman who disliked bad salad.
The impudence of that beggarly book-maker is

not endurable. You might have remarked a mild, gentlemanly young man in black; he came in just after us—an officer asked who he was? And Miss Carney, with unparalleled effrontery, curled up her nose, and said, ' Oh ! it's the Curate—dull creature—quite fit for church lumber.' "

" And the supper was nearly as droll as the melange," said Emily ; " the singing was ludicrous beyond description. The elderly gentleman who sang the comic song with all the gravity of Billington at an oratorio—I was all but in tears—"

" But," said O'Hara, " what tempted my poor friend, Driscol, to select ' Time has not thinned my flowing locks,'—when, to my certain knowledge, he has not had a hair on his head these ten years."

" And Miss Carney's cracked treble, as she shrieked—' See from ocean rising,'—to the accompanying growl of the cross-looking gentleman in the ' sooty wig,' as that arch Mr. Thornton called him across the table," said Emily.

" Oh! as to Thompson," observed O'Hara,

" really his horror of ' that Carney,' as he calls
her, is beyond concealment, and he never lets
an opportunity slip to teaze her ; but the best
of all was, when she was *doing modest*, and
mentioning that she rarely sang without an in-
strument, Thornton whispered a servant, who
returned with a Jew's-harp, and placed it on
the table with his compliments ; and, as if she
was not sufficiently enraged, he gravely congratulated her on her great command of voice,
for ' it was evident she could stop whenever she
pleased.' "

The melange, with its supper accompani-
ments, kept the party in a roar until the carriage passed through the gates of Castle Carra.

CHAPTER XIV.

The vulgar Irish are worse than the undaunted and un-
tamed Arabian, the devilish, idolatrous Turkoman, or the
moon-worshipping Carmines.

Lithgow's Travels.

THIRTY years have made a striking change in
the moral constitution of the Irish. The manners and habits of all classes have been reformed
and amended, and much of the barbarism which
tainted their feelings and degraded their native
virtues, has given way to the touch of refinement and civilization. Although " Green Erin"
has not forgotten the hospitality which distinguished her in " olden time," she has learned
to substitute social comfort for savage de-
bauchery. Excessive drinking is now banished
from the tables of the higher orders; and,
while a host of the last century would have
deemed himself disgraced in permitting his
guest to leave his hall without the assistance

Q 2

of his servants being indispensable, a better
ordered hospitality allows free indulgence to
individual fancy, and the visiter, when the wine
has lost its charm, is allowed a safe retreat, without endangering the loss of life or character.

A very different system was once observed
in the conduct of an Irish banquet. The
entertainer secured his company from retreating by locking them safely in :—" fast and
furious"—the drinking commenced ; and if an
unfortunate individual happened not to be provided with as potent a skull as the more gifted
bacchanals who surrounded him, he was either
obliged to sit quietly till he tumbled from the
chair, or absconded by the fortuitous opening
of a door or window, and even then, most probably, accompanied by the tender missive of a
decanter hurled at his head. These escapes
were, however, not generally to be effected ;
and, if this weak vessel had the good fortune
to escape prostration under the table, he had
still the chance of prostration on the field. If
the host was a choice spirit, he would most
probably resent this infraction on the laws of
Irish orgies, by parading the fugitive in the

morning, and repay the slight passed upon his port, by "tapping the claret" of the offender. It may easily be conceived that drunkenness was not the only ill consequence of those revels. The national spirit, wayward and ungovernable, was prepared to catch at any questionable word or opinion, as contrary interests actuated them. These were unfortunately often called forth in the moment of inebriety, and the consequences of a trifling misconception were fatal to the peace of families. All this is gone by—the memory of our fathers' follies is fresh; and while the chivalrous spirit of Ireland, shrinking from the semblance of insult, secures honour from violation, and delicacy from outrage, these sanguinary scenes of private encounter which were once so frequent, thank God, at this day but rarely occur.

That class of worthies, celebrated by such cognomens as " Five-bottle Jack"—" Fireaway Frank"—"Ten-duel Tom," are nearly extinct, and there are many high-spirited gentlemen, who have never yet been brought to the sod, on whose fathers the honour had been conferred, probably for the tenth time, before they had reached the years of their children. I have known a gentleman, whose son still preserves the weapons with which seventeen affairs of honour were concluded, (a registry is notched on the handle,) of which number nine fell to the lot of the proprietor, and the remainder were transacted by a few particular friends.

That these, and other similar habits, should have exposed the Irish to the charge of barbarism, was but just; but we must confess that their virtues (few as they might be) were not taken into account by their English neighbours when they formed an estimate of the national character. In the black catalogue of Pat's failings, his peculiarities were construed into crimes; and while the ebullitions of ill-directed courage were termed savage—while popular disapprobation was tortured to rebellion, and no name was considered sufficiently harsh, by which the vassal island should be designated— England forgot to look at herself, and, while she affected to despise the vices of the sister kingdom, she had within herself more of the barbarism she had denounced, without that shade of chivalry which shed a lustre even on the crimes for which she could find neither pity nor pardon. While every duel, riot, and rob- bery, occurring in Ireland, were journalized with faithful accuracy and copious colouring— as a set-off, we will presume, the next column was devoted to the more gratifying description of a bruising match, whose detail is given by the English editor with a satisfaction which in- dicates how gratifying the subject must be to the enlightened people who peruse his columns. Every round is critically remarked—each blow correctly examined—nor is this brutality con- fined to the mercenary wretches of the Fives Court—we are now and then treated with a " mill extraordinary" between a *fancy swell* and a big-boned Blacksmith. The *kiddy* alights from his tandem, gives the *ribbons* to his friend, doffs his *lily shallow* and *upper toggery*, and shows his *cambric* in a jiffy. Then follows a gratifying instance of the superiority of science over strength ; each round becomes more ex- hilarating—*Blackie*, though a *thorough-bred glutton*, gets unmercifully nobbed—the *swell's* hits are delightfully described as the battle proceeds. Blackie, in the course of compliments, receives a favour between his *nosegay-smeller* and *potato-trap*, which sends down his throat the *ivory part of his dinner set*. A right-hand facer from the amateur's *bunch of fives* hermetically seals his organ of *vision*, and thus politely saves him the trouble of looking through two eyes at once, till at last *a tie-up in the victualling office* completes the job—the swell slips on his *Poodle benjamin*, and rolls off in his *rattler*, amid the applauses of a delighted populace; while the knight of the anvil, less fortunate, modestly leaves the ground upon a shutter.   This is civilization!

It has been observed by some persons, who had intimately studied the situation of the country one hundred years ago, that the mortal arbitrament to which many of the disputes of the Irish were referred, were not without some advantage to meet the misfortunes inseparable from this summary decision of quarrels.   Parts of the kingdom were very thinly attended.   The remoter land proprietors lived in a state of feudal potency, and arrogated much of the same authority over the properties, and frequently the lives of their tenantry, which

the rights of vassalage had given their forefathers three hundred years before. These
personages, from the retired life in which they
were brought up, had little intercourse with
the world, and resolved all their thoughts
and actions to a standard founded on the customs of their ancestors, and not a little on
their sole will and discretion. If one of those
Chieftains happened to be of savage or violent
dispositions, nothing but the fear of a fellow-
potentate would prevent him from resorting
frequently to oppression and cruelty, and the
injured had no refuge but in the protection of
some rival Chief—this was rarely denied to the
suppliant; and, as the oppressor knew that a
call would be made upon him, which the honour
of Ireland rendered it impossible for him to
refuse, he frequently stopped short in his career
of tyranny. If he chose, however, to perse-
vere at all risks, he was generally removed
from the scene of life, a victim to his own bad
passions and misconduct. As the country became more open and civilized, these causes of
complaint, in a great measure, disappeared.
The laws became usefully and generally opera-

tive, and causes of aggravated oppression were seldom heard of.

There were other injuries, however, which custom continued to refer to personal decision. An Irish gentleman rarely troubled a court of law with libel or defamation ; he took justice into his own hands, and if that atonement which the code of honour authorised him to exact, was refused by the offending party, his character suffered so much in general estimation, that any thing short of excessive vengeance was fully satisfied by his degradation. Grievances of another kind, also, were referred to this sort of decision ; —any slight offered towards a lady set all her relations in a blaze ; and if a gentleman trifled with female affections, no special jury was empanelled, no florid advocate was employed, no pecuniary damages were awarded : a father, a brother, or a cousin to the remotest degree, was ever ready to do battle in the cause, and the delinquent paid with his best blood the forfeit of his indiscretion. We are, however, getting into the refinement of our English masters ; and, if the gentleman unties his purse-strings handsomely, his pistols may occasionally be dispensed with. But to return to my story.

It was late next morning when the family at Castle Carra assembled at the breakfast-table. Major O'Hara was reading the news-papers, when his son and the ladies entered to-gether. After the usual inquiries of the morn-ing, the Major handed a letter to Henry, and at the same time mentioned generally its con-tents. The sudden death of Sir Philip Blood, Member for the County of ———, was announ-ced ; and O'Hara observed, that in expectation of that event taking place, which had been long expected, from the late Member's delicate state of health, a large and respectable body of the Freeholders had communicated their wishes of putting him in nomination for their representation. He remarked, that were his own feelings to direct him, he should at once decline the intended honour, but he conceived himself called upon to assert the independence of the county, by acceding to their wishes, and offering himself as a candidate. Preliminary measures had been already arranged, and he should go off to Newbridge, to meet a Committee of the Electors, and (he continued with a smile) as a canvass would occupy him for some days, he must confide the seneschalship of his castle, and the defence of the fair dames who honoured it with their presence, to the heir-apparent. In a short time after, he ordered his horses, and took leave of his guests.

Lady Sarah was charmed with the idea of an election, with its balls and bustle—it would be quite delightful; and to prepare dresses of party-colours for herself and her fair daughter would occupy the intermediate time. Henry was now unavoidably the constant companion of Emily, and in riding and walking, the week of O'Hara's absence was consumed. Of his successful canvass, he frequently acquainted his son; and on the morning of his expected return, Henry rode into Newbridge to meet him, the ladies announcing their intention of following in the course of the day.

He had nearly reached the town when a young gentleman of the neighbourhood overtook him.

" Oh! Thornton, good morning. Well, what have you been doing since we met at the Melange?"

" Oh! curse the mummery of that crazy Cordwainer. I was sick for two days, by making Nugent and Scanlan drunk, hoping they would either fight themselves, break a mirror, splinter a vase, burn Miss Carney's MS. or Mrs. Glossin's wig, or do some notable mischief, but, confound them, they did not answer my expectations. And pray, gallant sir, what have you been doing? Turned sonnetteer, to eulogise an eyebrow. Come, we'll have you a contributor to the next Melange. " Stanzas on seeing Stella with a sprig of sweet briar;" " Sonnet to her slipper," or some amatory morceau. Are you gone, man? Is it all over with you? Are you, as we say in Ireland, kilt out and out?"

" I see, William, you are still the same hearty, careless fellow; but as we must make inquiries, how comes on your affair with Miss Nugent?"

" Pho! I will answer you in one word just as well as could be wished, all *pour passer le tems;* but as I am a liberal lover, if the dear creature could slay a Dragoon or Bombadier, I would hand her to the altar in per-

son, and say Amen when the Parson wished
them prosperity. But what will the sober
Citizens of Newbridge say, seeing orange and
pink riding ' party par pale ?' "

" Pshaw! Hang politics, you and I are not
likely to quarrel about such trifles."

" No—though I shall give a plumper against
the Major, in favour of a fellow I dislike ; but
then he's on the right side of the question.
Zounds ! ' Be there bears i' the town,' or what
the deuce is all this kick-up about? Forward."
And he spurred his horse on, accompanied by
his pink companion.

At the moment of their entering Newbridge,
a tin horn was sounded at the bottom of the
street, by the driver of a hackney chaise, which
a pair of feeble horses was endeavouring to
drag up the steep hill which led to the Loftus
Arms. The carriage was remarkable by a
flag flying from either window ; on its nearer
approach the banners were more distinctly revealed, and proved to be a couple of old worn-
out pocket handkerchiefs, extended on sallow
rods.

" It is Armstrong and his blackguard companion," said Thornton ; " ride up the street till we see them alight. By my hand, I'm half ashamed of my party. The fact is, my dear O'Hara, all the fighting men are on your side, Irvins, M'Donnells, and Moutrays ; and Lord Loftus, M'Cullogh, Nugent, and company, not feeling inclined to trust their valuable lives to the chance of a pistol shot, have wisely agreed to fight by proxy, and these precious scoundrels are engaged for one hundred pounds a piece, and their *grub*, for the election. But come along—there, the mob groan them and their tattered Barcelonas—and now out come the gemmen."

The chaise-door was opened, and the obsequious waiter was desired, with a tremendous execration, to " Hould the step steady."

" Your Honour's welcome, Mr. Armstrong."

" How are you, blast ye ?" replied the traveller.

" It's mad Archy, as his friends, the mob, call him," said Thornton ; " and, for Heaven's sake, look at his luggage.",

The person dignified by the title of mad Archy, was a stout, well set, middle-sized man, of forty, with small, grey, ferret eyes, and sandy hair; several scars across his countenance did not improve it, and a large nose was rendered more remarkable by the deep cut which bisected the bridge of that invaluable organ. His hands were occupied by a blackthorn stick and a case of pocket-pistols, and his whole luggage was under his arm, comprised within the inclosure of a purple cravat. After mad Archy had given his affectionate regards to the waiter, he paused, waiting for his companion in arms, who presently descended. This worthy was the opposite of his friend—a tall, thin, meagre wretch, with powdered hair, long cue, and silver spectacles. In point of property, he was nearly on a par, and as limited in chattels as his friend Archibald. A diminutive valise was consigned to the custody of the waiter, while himself took charge of a mahogany case, in which the gentleman's pistols (the tools of his trade) were deposited.

" What a pair," said Thornton, as they entered the Inn; " but you do not know them, Henry, nor their occupation. The first is an Attorney, but his practice is more at cockpits than courts of law; every horse-race within

many miles of him is carefully attended : as he
is a man of desperate and brutal habits, and
reckoned the best mob-leader in the north, they
have brought him here to command the banditti, which are ever the umpires of the qualifications for the fit representation of an Irish
County. He is also here for the purpose of
seconding his friend, who, in the event of his
pistols being required, would otherwise stand
a bad chance of obtaining any other person to
accompany him to the ground. The man is,
it is believed, subject to occasional derange-
ment ; and bad as he is, the other ruffian is ten
times worse. He is Captain Felton, alias
'Fire-away Phil ;' he tried several regiments,
but through bad taste, none of them could
agree with him, and he was obliged to retire on
half-pay to save his commission. He has killed
two or three certainly, and has fought duels
without number; you will see he will commence the business by insulting some gentleman of your party, of whom our leaders are
afraid ; and, if he be unfortunate enough to go
out with this savage, the chances of his death
are pretty certain. But here is your carriage

coming in, and that lovely creature in full pink.
Damme, I'll slip the orange cockade out of my
hat, raise the pink, and turn renegado, if she
will only give me one smile of the thousands
which are bestowed on a nameless Cavalier.
Come, to your duty, man,—I must be off,—
Orange for ever!" and away Thornton bolted.

The Castle Carra carriage was soon hailed
by the pink party, of which the town was almost entirely composed; and a very different
reception attended their entry from that of the
last vehicle; the huzzas of the mob, the beauty
of the females in the carriage, the curvetting
of the handsome bays, which, startled by the
cheering of the populace, were tossing their
pink rosettes about, brought young and old to
the doors. Henry's cheek flushed with conscious pride, as he heard his own name coupled
by the crowd with that of Emily De Clifford:
never had she looked so lovely, and never was
party colour seen to more advantage. On the
carriage reaching the inn, before the door of
which the hack which conveyed mad Andy and
the gallant Captain stood, with its tawdry rags
yet dangling from the windows, the "canaille"

in a second tattered them to shreds, and saluted the worthy proprietors, who were quietly discussing brandy and water at an open window, with a shower of dead cats and offal, which rendered a rapid retreat unavoidable. None lamented their discomfiture; and two English bagmen, whom this respectable couple had unceremoniously kicked out of the room, and tossed their pattern-books and portmanteaus down stairs after them, looked on with a satisfaction that would have fully compensated for any thing short of the loss of their Bourdeaux, which these ruthless intruders were despatching with perfect complacency, before the regards of the " Bourgeois" obliged them to retire.

R 2

CHAPTER XV.

Pretty rebel! where's the jest
Of wearing Orange in thy breast ?
When that bosom doth disclose
The whiteness of the Rebel-rose.

Impromptu.

In the afternoon Henry was leaving Newbridge, and in passing the shop of the chief
milliner, stopped to admire the prudence of the
" Marchande de Modes," for with due consideration she had gratified the Republicans by
adorning one window with pink ; while its
neighbour, with proper attention to the Aristocracy, was bedizened with flashy orange.
Miss Moreen was determined to keep up a running fire with both parties; and although a
pious Methodist, and consequently one of the
children of light, she proved in all matters ap-
pertaining to the mammon of unrighteousness,
that she was no fool in her generation. O'Hara

was riding from the repository of fashion, when hearing his name pronounced, he perceived in the Milliner's drawing-room window his fair friend, Lady Constantia Loftus. " Come up, pink knight," said her ladyship. ". Miss Moreen will allow you to enter her forbidden precincts ; and here, among silks and satins, relate your adventures since your departure, which happened some period, I believe, during the last century."

Henry despatched his horse to the Inn, and Miss Moreen, on hearing her fair customer's invitation, was already simpering at the door to conduct the pink gallant to that important apartment where those tempting articles, stated to be " direct from London and Dublin," were exhibiting to captivating advantage.

" Moreen, may I trouble you to send to the inn, and desire my servants not to bring the carriage for half an hour."

" An hour, if you please," said Miss Moreen. " Old friends, like your Ladyship and Mr. O'Hara, must have much to speak of, and you need not be afraid of interruption, for none but particular friends are admitted here."

" What a considerate creature it is," said
Lady Constantia, with much archness, as the
pious Milliner retired. "And now, good Sir,
—Pshaw! Henry, we are too old for kissing.
Heigh ho! how time flies—you are twenty-
two, and that impertinent Debrett makes me
nineteen in his Peerage. And now that I have
an opportunity to scold, was it kind to put me
off with one formal visit, and that too when
surrounded with Goths and Vandals, which
prevented me from asking a single question ?"

" Why, my dear Lady Constantia, you have
been but a few days at home, and assuredly I
did not let a moment pass when I heard of your
return, until I rode to Loftus-Hall ; and you
know Lord Loftus, and Monteville, and my
father, are at present more opposed than ever ;
and cold looks and cold greeting would not be
agreeable, where in earlier, and I fear, happier days, (Lady Constantia sighed deeply,) I
passed many a sunny hour."

" Nay, Henry, don't talk of old times as if
those days were never to return. But what a
long tour you have made ; and, mercy on me,
how you are grown. For Heaven's sake don't

listen to the women, or they will certainly turn your brain with flattery. But what have you been doing? Where have you wandered? Were you learning the art of love, or the art of war? Or probably, as is the case with most of your worthy countrymen, practising both trades, as the opposite apothecary adds to his name surgeon and man-mid— ? But, Lord bless me, what was I reading?" and she threw down her glass, and blushed.

"Well, dear Constance, you shall hear my travels at the first ball we meet; but, now I want to ask you some questions about certain matters that rumour carried even to parts beyond the four seas of Britain. Was it true that the High Sheriff— ?"

"Oh! name him not; it was dotage, I presume. But, why ask me?"

"Because in that case I should have forbidden the banns, even although necessitated to take charge of you for life."

"The gratitude I feel for the distinguished honour conferred on me, as I overheard my father say to the tallow-chandler at the corner, whom he was cajoling for his 'vote and interest,' as the candle-maker termed it; but indeed, Henry, I do think you would not have allowed your old playmate to be sacrificed to a brute; and between ourselves, my father and brother have been rather sulky since; but my mamma had too much pity or too much pride to join in the conspiracy, and, thanks to my aunt's twenty thousand pounds, I was enabled to assert my independence, and reject that upstart."

Miss Moreen was perfectly right in her calculation; a long hour elapsed, and neither of the parties remembered the carriage. The coachman thought that the milliner's maid would be despatched again when he was wanted, and therefore, although attached to orangeism and aristocracy, in proof of his liberality, settled himself in the ale-house with a couple of pink footmen to talk politics, drink beer, and, if possible, convince them of the error of their opinions. The town clock at last startled the occupants of Miss Moreen's sofa. "Henry, give me your arm to the inn, and, as it would be treason, if my sire or his son met me without the badge of party, here I shall affix my colours,"—and she pinned an orange rosette in her bonnet. " And as we shall be frequently in town during the ensuing contest, whenever an hour hangs heavily, re-collect Moreen's drawing-room ; and believe me, Harry, that whatever alteration political discordancy may create between the name of Loftus and O'Hara, the feelings of our younger days (at least I shall answer for my own) will never be forgotten."

They had now reached the street, and the pink cavalier, with the fair Aristocrat hanging on his arm, left the Milliner of doubtful po-litics, but indubitable piety, to meet the car-riage at the Loftus Arms.

On turning the corner of the street, the pink and orange pedestrians suddenly confronted Lord Loftus and his party, engaged in can-vassing the citizens of Newbridge. Their un-expected appearance, and the evident amity of the younger branches of the rival houses, asto-nished the whole group. Lord Monteville coloured on seeing his sister and her escort ; however, suppressing his feelings, he came forward and presented his hand, which was readily accepted. " Constance, my dear, I really thought you had left Newbridge long ago. Your mamma will think you are lost."

" Oh! no, Monteville, I met O'Hara at Moreen's, and have been endeavouring to persuade him to give you his support." Henry smiled. " And the truth is, he seems the only idler in town, and therefore I have enlisted him ; but I perceive you are wanting in the tin-shop. I'll tell you how to gain him. Look at the blowzy cross-looking orange-woman in the window, and the gawky girl, peering over her mother's shoulder, as if she was afraid you were going to rob the shop. Tell him, good man," (she continued with mock gravity) " that his spouse is amiable and comely—that he has ' a daughter passing fair,' and that you hope from the marked sensibility of his own countenance, that he will assist you with his grave advice as to the best method of putting down the Papists, or paying the debts of the nation."

" Go, go, Constance ; you would lose me my election with your nonsense, if I don't keep you in Loftus-Hall."

" Then to do that, remove the wheels from

the carriage and lame the horses; for, by all
that's curious, I must and will attend the election as regularly as the returning officer."

" O'Hara, do take her away."

" And then for the tinman," cried his lively
sister, as she nodded to Lord Monteville, and
proceeded through the canvassers who followed
him. Among the number was M‘Cullogh;
he drew himself up, and attempted to look
indifferent; but the haughty bow of Lady
Constantia, as she scarcely acknowledged his
humble salute, and the proud movement of
O'Hara, as he slightly touched his hat, conveyed that cold contempt which wounds more
deeply than the severest language. The orange
party were still in the tin-shop, when the pinks
appeared in full force at the upper end of the
street.

" What will become of me now," said Lady
Constantia; " my retreat is cut off—are your
friends quiet, Henry? or will my luckless
rosette occasion my ruin; but as I see your
father in the centre, I trust my life at least
will be safe."

What astonished the ultras amused the pinks,

and O'Hara, stepping from the crowd, came forward with a smile—" Well, who has succeeded? Which is the proselyte? Or, like the priest and parson, have you become mutual converts?"

" Why I have shaken Henry undoubtedly, but truly I must strike at higher game; shall I try my influence on you?"

" No, dear Constance, I am too old an offender; whatever chance a lovely girl has with kindred youth, she has little with gnarled, crabbed age."

" Come, you shall not give yourself a worse character than you deserve; I know you are not so bad as you would make me believe, and now to try it."

She plucked a lily from the hat of a passing boy, and shredding a leaf from the stalk, twined it in the bow of ribbon which was attached to the Major's breast. O'Hara smiled, as he pressed the hand of the playful girl. " There shall it remain, dear Constance, to prove that old affections are not to be disturbed by party— there shall your bright leaf rest, and though its livelier hue may mock its paler rival, yet the remembrance of the hand which placed it there shall preserve it inviolate. But am I sentimentalizing with a giddy girl, while Monteville secures the electors, and gains the ' golden opinions' of—"

" Tinmen and Tallow-chandlers," said Lady Constantia.

" Go, tempter," and he playfully patted her cheek, while she gracefully saluted the pink politicians (who were all respectfully uncovered), and stepped into the carriage.

" Adieu, Henry ; I mean to be in town tomorrow—remember Miss Moreen's."

The election commenced on the following morning ; crowds of country gentlemen came fast in, with their respective flocks of freeholders. The usual formalities were observed—the candidates proposed in one bad speech, and seconded in another, and the polling opened. Five days passed over, and the general history of an Irish election will describe them. Clamour and confusion—prevarication and perjury occupied the day ; riot, drunkenness, and disorder, consumed the night. Old registries were ransacked, and persons who for years

before had been reposing peaceably in their
graves, good-naturedly got up on the occasion
to vote for Lord Monteville.   Every artifice
was resorted to;   money plentifully used to
procure the venal, and threats and promises to
induce the better classes.   The contest was
carried on with unusual bitterness, as the ordinary irritability of opposition was heightened by
political rancour.   From the violence of party,
O'Hara was anxious to keep Henry as much at
home as possible, while the son, alarmed for his
parent's safety, seldom left the town.

On the sixth day, an attempt was made by
the Aristocrats to get a priest personated.
The fellow who enacted *the Clargy* appeared
arrayed in a huge bushy wig, and coat of dingy
black, and swore without hesitation that he
was Father Anthony O'Toole; but, unluckily
for the reverend representative of the departed
friar, his brother happened to be present, and
declared that the said Anthony must have been
badly used, as they had buried him fifteen years
before.   This scandalous subornation drew forth
strong reprobation from O'Hara, which Captain Felton, who was watching an opportunity,

contrived to turn to account; for, in course of
an altercation which ensued, he gave a direct
lie to the Major, and completed the insult
by striking him in the face with an orange.
At this time Henry was sitting with Lady
Loftus and her daughter at Miss Moreen's,
and hearing some noise in the street, learned
from a passenger the outrage which had been
offered to his father. In vain Lady Loftus implored him to be patient. In vain Constantia,
with pale cheek and faltering voice, entreated
him not to be rash. He bounded down the stairs,
and in a minute was mingled with the crowd.

The Castle Carra tenantry were in a terrific uproar, threatening death and destruction
to Felton and his party; and having just then
found that the object of vengeance had eluded
their fury, by escaping through a side-door,
their madness was not to be controlled.
Henry suspecting that the Captain would retreat to the Loftus Arms, and remembering
that a narrow lane led to the inn-yard, and
saved the long detour of the public street,
went in pursuit of the ruffian. On emerging
from the alley, he perceived him retreating to

the inn, and snatching a whip from a lounging post-boy, he seized him in his powerful grasp and proceeded to exercise him without mercy. Nothing but a sally of his friends from the Loftus Arms, prevented him from rivalling the fate of Marsyas of old, and suffering death from flagellation ; however, before the rescue was effected, a challenge to fight in half an hour was given and accepted.

An election terminating without a few duels, would then have been anomalous, and country gentlemen, when they left their homes to select their representative, had the precaution to provide themselves with approved weapons. Henry, therefore, had no difficulty in procuring pistols and an experienced friend ; and Mr. Moutray promised to call on him at his private lodgings in due time, and conduct him to the ground.

Robert Moutray was a gentleman of ancient family and small estate, attached to no profession, and residing where his fathers had lived for centuries. He was an honourable man, and generally respected ; and, from a particular fondness for politics and bustle, held a place among the county leaders far above what his small fortune would warrant him to look to. He was a zealot in politics; and, as he entered heart and soul into whatever cause he adopted, from his determined courage and unwearied ardour, joined to a caustic method of expression, he was generally distinguished by the sobriquet of " *Bitter Bob*." Although past the meridian of life, and the father of a numerous family, his active, political habits were unsubdued by years, and he accepted the invitation with pleasure, to accompany Henry to the field.

Short as the intervening time was, young O'Hara wished anxiously for its accomplishment; he hoped the affair would terminate before his father was apprized of his situation, as he could well fancy a parent's sufferings while his child was exposed to danger, and his fate still rested in the balance. He tried to reach his own retired lodgings; but to pass Miss Moreen's without being observed was impossible, as Lady Constantia was leaning from the window, apparently watching for his return.

" I hope, my dear O'Hara, this unpleasant business has been exaggerated; surely the Major would think too much of rank and character to notice a hired bully?"

" Oh! fear nothing, Constance, for my father; I shall take care that he does not come in contact with that bravo."

" But how, Henry—not by"—(she became agitated)—" not by quarrelling yourself?" and she turned her keen glance upon him.

" Oh! no," he replied, with a smile; " I have only to turn the cudgels of Castle Carra against the doughty Captain."

" Would to Heaven he was drummed out of the county; but, indeed, Henry, I was miserable about you—I mean your father; and, as I had a better chance of hearing news here, I declined going with mamma to make a sick visit to the Rector's lady."

The conversation took another turn, and Henry spoke with tolerable ease on indifferent subjects, but frequent reference to his watch, and restless looks to the street, betrayed the anxiety he was so careful to conceal.

" Nay, O'Hara, tell me not that something momentous is not occupying your thoughts— I see it, I remark the altered manner."

" Constance, believe me that I have little wish to leave you; but, in fact, I have an appointment relative to election arrangements which must force me, although reluctantly, to bid you good bye for this day."

" And shall I see you *to-morrow ?*" and the emphasis she laid on to-morrow, struck Henry to the heart.

" Oh yes," he replied, with assumed gaiety, " certainly; and see, there comes my friend."

" Your friend ! What! is *Bitter Bob* engaged in this business ? Henry, for God's sake ! are you involved in any quarrel—tell me truly —I am interested, deeply interested as I would be for my brother. And Heavens! there is Surgeon D'Arcy with Moutray."

" Why, Constance, the truth is, Moutray is going to fight, and I am to be his friend. Adieu, dear Constance,—dear sister,—I will come to you in an hour."

" Do—do," she faintly replied, as she sank upon the couch.

" Hark! Moutray calls me;" and leaving
the apartment, he mounted his friend's gig.

As the vehicle started, he looked for a moment to the window—his young friend had
risen from the sofa ; he saw her face—it was
agitated ; the momentary look could not be
mistaken, and O'Hara must have been dull
indeed, had he not suspected that Lady Constantia loved him.   If his thoughts dwelt upon
this gentle subject, they were soon interrupted
by Moutray's entering on the business they
were hastening to transact.   He coolly gave
him his directions and advice, entering with
great *sang froid* into discussions on distances
and signals.   In a few minutes the gig stopped,
and Moutray remarking they were first upon
the ground, quietly unlocked the pistol-case,
and produced the necessary apparatus.

The place where affairs of honour were
usually decided was within a short distance of
the town.   It was a level meadow, surrounded
by rising grounds, and afforded ample accommodation for the hundreds who had flocked to
witness the decision of the quarrel with the
same composure with which they would have

crowded to a cock-fight. Three or four of
O'Hara's friends were waiting for him, and
they accompanied him through the spectators,
who were all decorated with the insignia of
their respective parties, until they reached the
scene of action—it was the centre of the field,
and marked by a gentle undulation of the sur-
face. Here several lives had been forfeited at
the shrine of mistaken honour, and a few stones
pointed out the exact spot where one had lately
fallen. At this little monument Henry awaited
the approach of Felton and his friends : they
were not long absent, and the seconds retired
a few paces to arrange preliminaries.

If there be a moment when the duellist feels
agitated, it is at this trying time. Amidst the
dead silence of the spectators, the stepping of
the allotted distance, and all the usual preparations for the affair, were quickly transacted.
Henry felt neither trepidation nor dismay, and
his antagonist looked on with equal indifference ; their feelings, however, were very dissimilar—with one, a chivalrous devotion had
sent the son to battle for the parent, and sub-

stitute his own person to protect that of his
gallant father. The other's, was the cold-
blooded hardihood of a practised homicide;
he stood as he had frequently done before, and
without a pang of remorse, prepared to hurry
his youthful opponent from existence.

The seconds had assigned the respective situation to each principal, when a buzz among the
distant crowd turned the attention of the parties to the road, and a horseman was seen advancing rapidly. Some persons having called
out " the Sheriff is coming," the seconds instantly placed the pistols in their friends' hands,
retired, and gave the signal. Henry fired
without hesitation, but Felton deliberated for
a few moments. " Shame—murder," began
to be muttered when he discharged his pistol—
the ball passed through Henry's hat, and Felton, with a savage oath, muttered something
to mad Andy, accounting for the failure of his
fire. The weapons were again prepared, when
Thornton came up and implored O'Hara to
aim steadily, and not let the ruffian take his
life. Felton's conduct, however, had already

awakened him to a sense of his danger, and he observed him cautiously while awaiting the expected signal.

The horseman had now approached sufficiently near to be distinguished, and one glance told him that it was his father. With a strong exertion he mastered the agitation his presence caused, and coolly prepared for the moment of action.

Major O'Hara was on the hustings when a rumour reached him that his son had gone out with Felton. With a groan of horror he rushed into the street, and called loudly for his horse. A young gentleman instantly tendered his, and the distracted parent gallopped to the scene of combat. The crowds on the road made way for him ; and, as he reached the high ground that overlooked the field, a discharge of pistols told him that all might *now* be over ! A man standing on a high wall, called out, that " both were on their legs." He rode madly on, if possible to prevent the fire from being repeated. His appearance, however, precipitated what he was so anxious to prevent :— again a murmur of the mob told that the par-

ties were ready—and again there was an awful
silence. His further progress was impeded by
a gate, and he sprang from his horse to open it
—at that instant the pistols were discharged.
O'Hara's limbs almost failed him, his eyes
grew dim, while a kind of murmuring groan
burst from the crowd. "He's down, by G—d!"
cried one of the spectators. He staggered for
support against the gate-pier. "Felton's done
for!" roared another voice exultingly; and
such had been, indeed, the result. Henry escaped unhurt, and his savage opponent was
stretched upon the field.

END OF VOL. I.

LONDON:
PRINTED BY W. CLOWES,
Northumberland-Court.

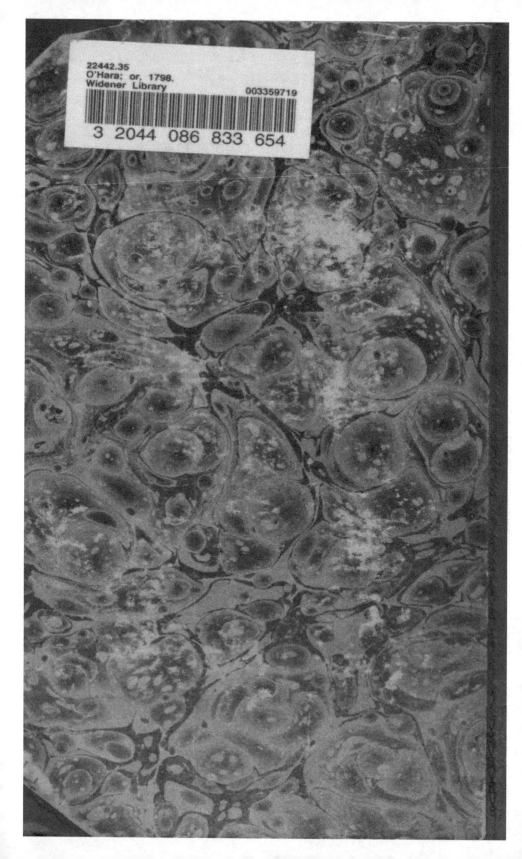

Check Out More Titles From HardPress Classics Series In this collection we are offering thousands of classic and hard to find books. This series spans a vast array of subjects – so you are bound to find something of interest to enjoy reading and learning about.

Subjects:
Architecture
Art
Biography & Autobiography
Body, Mind &Spirit
Children & Young Adult
Dramas
Education
Fiction
History
Language Arts & Disciplines
Law
Literary Collections
Music
Poetry
Psychology
Science
…and many more.

Visit us at www.hardpress.net

CPSIA information can be obtained
at www.ICGtesting.com
Printed in the USA
BVHW091904220819
556561BV00021B/4799/P